CHRISTOPHER COLUMBUS'S JEWISH ROOTS

CHRISTOPHER COLUMBUS'S JEWISH ROOTS

Jane Frances Amler

JASON ARONSON INC.

Northvale, New Jersey
London

The author gratefully acknowledges permission to quote from the following sources:

Admiral of the Ocean Sea: A Life of Christopher Columbus by Samuel Eliot Morison. Copyright © 1942 by Samuel Eliot Morison. Copyright © renewed 1970 by Samuel Eliot Morison. By permission of Little, Brown and Company

A History of the Marranos by Cecil Roth. Copyright © 1974 Sepher-Hermon Press, Inc. By permission of Sepher-Hermon Press, Inc.

Production Editor: Judith D. Cohen
Editorial Director: Muriel Jorgensen

This book was set in 12/15 Souvenir by
Alpha Graphics of New Hampshire
and printed and bound by Haddon Craftsmen
of Pennsylvania.

Library of Congress Cataloging-in-Publication Data

Amler, Jane Frances.
    Christopher Columbus's Jewish roots / by Jane Frances Amler.
        p.   cm.
    Includes bibliographical references and index.
    ISBN 0-87668-586-6
    1. Columbus, Christopher Relations with Jews.   2. Columbus,
Christopher—Family.   3. Jews—Spain—History.   4. America—
Discovery and exploration—Spanish.   I. Title.
E112.A45   1991
970.01'5—dc20
[B]   91-16694

Manufactured in the United States of America. Jason Aronson Inc. offers books and cassettes. For information and catalog write to Jason Aronson Inc., 230 Livingston Street, Northvale, New Jersey 07647.

For Larry,
Scott, and Michael

CONTENTS

ACKNOWLEDGMENT

My interest in this subject grew out of a desire to research and record our family's rich Jewish heritage, a desire instilled in me by my mother and inherited from my father, a direct descendant of Don Isaac Abravanel. I would like to thank Linsey Abrams for her many hours of editorial help and inspirational advice, and I am indebted to Arthur Kurzweil for the critical support he has provided. Judy Cohen and Muriel Jorgensen were instrumental in helping me see this book through to publication, and I wish to express my sincere appreciation. I thank my family and friends for their love and encouragement. While conducting research for this book, I found discrepancies in historic dates as well as a number of different spellings for proper names and places. If any factual errors were made on my part, please note that every effort was made to consider documented facts over speculation. My reconstruction of history was culled from English texts, and an effort was made to infuse the subject with an imaginative spark of life in order to capture a sense of the tumultuous times in which Columbus lived.

1

CRISTOBAL COLON—ITALIAN OR SPANISH-JEWISH DESCENT?

1451–1506

Portrait of Christopher Columbus, attributed to Sebastiano del Piombo (1485–1547). Reprinted by permission of the Metropolitan Museum of Art, Gift of J. Pierpont Morgan, 1900. (00.18.2)

And thus, having expelled the Jews from all your kingdoms and dominions, in the same month of January Your Highnesses commanded me that with a sufficient fleet I should go to said parts of India; and for that purpose granted me great honours and ennobled me so that henceforth I should be styled Don and should be Grand Admiral of the Ocean Sea and Viceroy and Governor-General in perpetuity of the Islands and terra firma.[1]

—Christopher Columbus

Boabdil the Young handed the key to Alhambra and all of Granada to King Ferdinand and Queen Isabella on January 2, 1492. Sitting upon caparisoned horses, the king and queen were surrounded by a host of knights whose armor gleamed in the sun and whose colorful banners hailed from England, France, and Germany. All waited breathlessly during the exchange of hostage children, including Boabdil's firstborn son. The ten year reconquista to oust the Moors from Spain was complete. Having fought for Jaen, and having laid siege to Malaga, Baza, and finally Granada (the southernmost kingdom of roses and jasmine), the Most Catholic Monarchs were victorious in this last great crusade.

Standing in the crowd, a solitary, forty-one-year-old Christopher Columbus witnessed the surrender. He had left

Genoa, city of his birth, and had been shipwrecked in Portugal, where he most probably conceived his dream of sailing west to find the East. In Portugal he had petitioned King Joao II to grant him his expedition. When he was rejected there, he had traveled to Spain, hoping to find a royal sponsor. He had waited six years while the reconquista was being fought and now, as he witnessed the key to Alhambra being handed to King Ferdinand, he must have hoped that his dream would become a reality. Columbus would have recognized the royal party: the young Prince Don Juan astride his horse just behind the king, the commander-general Ponce de Leon and the man many called the third king, Cardinal Pedro Gonzales de Mendoza. Columbus saw the last great caliph to sit upon the throne of Alhambra turn with his entourage and ride away, closing a seven-hundred-year period of Moslem rule in Spain. Cardinal Mendoza rode into Alhambra and raised the cross along with the royal banner of the castle and the lion; the reconquista was complete.

Shortly after the fall of Granada, the royal counsel appointed to study Columbus's proposal rejected it. The royal coffers had been depleted by the crusade—there was no money for this risky enterprise. Stunned by the rejection, Columbus prepared to take his proposal to Charles VIII of France. He was riding his mule across the Bridge of Pinos when a messenger from the queen overtook him, recalling him to the royal court in Santa Fe, a newly completed Christian town just outside of Alhambra. The Catholic Monarchs had changed their minds and were going to finance his expedition. Within the period of time it had taken Columbus to pack and ride out, a plan to expel the Jews had been conceived. While royal treasurers were searching for a number of ways to finance Columbus's enterprise, King

Ferdinand contemplated using the monies confiscated from Jewish property to refill the royal coffers. This potential new source of funds must have played a part in Ferdinand's infamous decision to expel the Jews.

* * *

In 1492 there were over three hundred thousand Jews living in Spain. Having lived on the Iberian Peninsula (Spain and Portugal) for over a thousand years, the Jews were now, suddenly, given three months in which to leave. The Jews had lived in what is now called the "Golden Age" of Spain. They had been, for the most part, protected by the kings who valued their knowledge as treasurers, doctors, lawyers, and craftsmen in many fields. While they enjoyed the protection of the kings, there were always elements of the society (within the church and among the noblemen) that flared against them in terrible acts of rioting. Rules and regulations were often put into effect that severely limited and controlled Jewish lives. Despite these restrictions, the Jews had flourished for hundreds of years and were deeply entrenched in Spanish life. While the Catholic Monarchs desired complete unification of church and state, the expulsion of the Jews was inextricably intertwined with Ferdinand's desire to keep Columbus from his archenemy, King Charles VIII of France. From the time Ferdinand was a prince in Aragon (a northern Spanish kingdom), he had battled the French for the province of Roussillon. Ferdinand had even ridden off to Roussillon during the Spanish-Portuguese war in order to fight against Charles.

In January of 1492 Ferdinand had been informed by his royal counsel, which had studied Columbus's proposal, that the mathematical estimation of the distance was grossly short, and that while it might be possible to reach the Indies by sailing west, there were grave doubts that the winds could carry the ships home. So at first King Ferdinand rejected Columbus's proposal. But under the advice of his treasurers, Ferdinand began to realize that the kingdom that first discovered a water route to the Indies would become the most powerful in all Christendom. It came down to a matter of being able to finance a voyage of great risk. King Ferdinand was prepared to go to any lengths to keep Columbus's enterprise away from Charles, even prepared to expel the Jews.

* * *

Who was Christopher Columbus? Certainly many nationalities have claimed him as their own: Spanish, Portuguese, French, German, English, Greek, and Armenian. The controversy concerning Columbus's origins continues between Italian and Spanish Columbian scholars. The Italian proponents have carefully documented the fact that Columbus was born in Genoa and lived his life as a faithful Catholic, while the Spanish scholars claim that Columbus was of Spanish-Jewish origin. In his biography of Columbus, *Admiral of the Ocean Sea*, Samuel Eliot Morison (a respected proponent of the Italian point of view) writes that "there is no mystery about the birth, family or race of Christopher Columbus. He was born in the ancient city of Genoa sometime between August 25 and the end of October, 1451, the son and grandson of woolen weavers who had been living in the various towns of the Genoese Republic for at least three generations."[2] Genoese documents referring to Cristoforo Colombo at various times during this early life still exist. All the scholars agree that he was born in Genoa and lived his early years there. But even Morison went on to write that "the Discoverer's remote ancestors doubtless belonged to other races than the Italian."[3] The equally respected Spanish scholar, Salvador de Madariaga, in his biography, *Christopher Columbus, Being the Life of The Very Magnificent Lord Don Cristobal Colon*, claimed that Columbus's other ancestry was not so remote as Morison would have the reader believe. Madariaga tried to trace the Colombo family back to Catalonia and suggested that as a Spanish Jewish family they were driven out of Catalonia during the 1391 anti-Jewish riots and then made their way into the Italian city states.

The medieval world of the late fourteenth century was a chaotic time when disease and hunger were constant factors created by war, poor harvests, and heavy taxes. With the unsanitary conditions of waste and garbage spilling out into the muddy streets, and rats and mice milling about, the Black Death and the plague spread rapidly, depopulating whole villages and towns. In turn, this created fear and distrust, causing superstitions to grow and ripen. The Jews were often blamed for illness, death, and bad luck. They had been expelled from England in 1290, France in 1306 and again in 1394. Because of Jewish religious and cultural differences, Jews were forced to live within the confines of their own quarters in the Spanish kingdoms and were given the unpleasant jobs of tax collectors and usurers (Usury was relegated to Jews because it was prohibited within the Catholic Church.).

In Castile and Aragon (the two largest Christian kingdoms in the Spains), the situation for the Jews was just as confining. When King Juan I of Castile died in October 1390, he left the regency of his infant son, Enrique III, to his queen, Leonora. Her confessor, Fray Ferrant Martinez, had been preaching vicious anti-Semitic sermons against the Jews. With the ascent of the queen, Martinez's vitriolic preaching reached a frenzied pitch, instilling such hatred that mobs attacked the Jewish quarter in Seville on March 15 and June 4, 1391, murdering 4,000 men, women, and children. The ones who survived agreed to convert. This rampage of violence, murder, and rape spread throughout the Spains. In the towns of Ecija and Carmona the Jewish communities were destroyed. The Jewish quarter in Cordova was burned to the ground. The Jews of Toledo suffered a massacre.[4]

Spreading like fire, the massacres extended into the kingdom of Aragon, then Catalonia, a northern province bordering France and the Mediterranean Sea. Though King Juan I of Aragon tried to stop the massacres, terrible rioting took place in Valencia and Barcelona in July 1391. The great Jewish scholar Cecil Roth estimates that over 50,000 Jews lost their lives during this reign of terror.[5] Some Jews chose conversion over death, and the Church accepted them into the fold. As Yitzhak Baer notes, "It appears that many Jews were converted in the course of those days. . . . All the Jewish communities of Catalonia, both urban and rural were thus destroyed or impoverished."[6] Madariaga suggests that during these riots the Jewish Colombo family, living in Catalonia, converted in order to save their lives and then fled Spain. Indeed, out of this terrible holocaust the Conversos (converted Jews) arose in great numbers throughout all of the Iberian Peninsula.

If Columbus was born into a Converso family, the family name might give some clue to his extraction. Certainly he was never addressed by the name Christopher Columbus in his lifetime. The Genoa records refer to Domenico Colombo, his wife Susanna Fontanarossa, and their sons Cristoforo (Christopher), Bartholomeo (Bartholomew), and

Giacomo (Diego) and at least one daughter, Bianchinetta. Morison (p. 9) notes that the records concerning the Colombos date back to Columbus's grandfather, Giovanni, and this fits the Spanish suggestion that this grandfather, in a life saving effort, converted in the 1391 Catalonian riots, and then fled into northern Italy. The Spanish form of Colombo is Colon, the name Columbus used when he was presented to King Ferdinand and Queen Isabella. His use of his family's old name was so significant that Columbus's son and biographer, Don Ferdinand Colon, wrote, "To conform it with the fatherland where he went to live and to take a new state, he filed down the word to make it conform with the old and thus called himself Colon; this leads me to believe that just as most of his things were worked out of some kind of mystery, so in what pertains to the variation in his name and surname there is sure to be some mystery."[7] Don Ferdinand states that Colon was the family name of old, and that once in Spain his father reverted to the original name. This sentence of Don Ferdinand's gives credence to the Spanish scholars who suggest the Colons were living in Catalonia in the 1390s.

To add further light to this argument, Cecil Roth investigated the name "Colombo" and found that in Hebrew it means "Jonah" or "dove." Roth states that in the northern Italian provinces "a man who signed his Hebrew letters Colon was invariably known in the outside world by the name 'Colombo,' which was the easiest approximation that a liquid-voiced Italian would reach."[8] While there were non-Jews by the name of Colon in Spain, it is significant that Columbus reverted to that name in his audiences with the king and queen. He was also addressed by that name in the Capitulations that granted him his many honors and titles when he discovered land on his expedition. In fact, he wanted the name Colon to be recorded in perpetuity, the name his children, Don Ferdinand and Don Diego, took with them to their graves. Perhaps Don Ferdinand's mystery concerning his father's name was simply the family's way of hiding their Jewish extraction. Madariaga, Roth, and Baer all suggest that the mystery that surrounds the Colombo or Colon family fades if one considers that Columbus would have had to hide his Jewish extraction from the Inquisition.

In 1492 Spain, Columbus would have been keenly aware of the ever-present Spanish Inquisition, which had been active for more than ten years. In 1483, Fray Tomas Torquemada, Queen Isabella's childhood confessor, was appointed Grand Inquisitor of the Inquisition. Under his terrible reign the number of people investigated, tortured, and burned at the stake dramatically increased. Once the church had confessions of heresy (of having secretly practiced their former Jewish religion), usually obtained through torture, the victims were burned in acts of faith or autos de fé. Since Church doctrine did not permit the shedding of blood as punishment for heretics, death by fire did not implicate the Church in any forbidden act, so this was an acceptable means of putting heretics to death. During the six years Columbus had lived in Spain, hundreds of Conversos as well as Jews died at the stake. If Columbus was indeed of Jewish extraction, he was walking a thin line between realizing his dream to sail to India and keeping his background from the prying eyes of the Inquisition. It is possible that Columbus faced greater danger within Spain than on the uncharted high seas.

* * *

Starting with the Spanish-Jewish name of Colon, the arguments supporting the belief that Columbus was of Jewish extraction begin to grow. In the same infamous year of 1391, the Conversos of Majorca were ordered to learn the art of weaving, an art the Mediterranean Jews were well known for, as were the Jews of Catalonia.[9] In his youth Columbus was only a carder of wool, but his father, Domenico, was a weaver. Morison writes that

> Giovanni Colombo, the Discoverer's paternal grandfather, was a weaver of woolen cloth from the village of Moconesi . . . a seaport about twenty miles east of Genoa. . . . By 1440, . . . Domenico (Columbus's father) has become a master weaver, and hired a house just inside the Porta dell'Olivella, the eastern gate of Genoa. About 1445 he married Susanna Fontanarossa, daughter of a weaver.[10]

Weaving was one of the few occupations open to the Jews. While there has been some question as to Susanna's Jewish background, it is interesting to note that she, too, was from a family of weavers.

From the twelfth to the fifteenth centuries, Jews were weavers, map makers, makers of nautical instruments, bookbinders, blacksmiths, tax collectors, carpenters, astronomers, merchants in the fur, cloth, silk, and spice trades, physicians, mathematicians, shoemakers, tanners, horse and mule traders, scholars, and teachers. Of these professions the Columbus family was known to have participated in weaving, bookbinding, and map making, while Christopher made use of astronomy on his voyages. Whereas these coincidences in themselves do not prove that the Columbus family was of Jewish origin, it is significant that they found the means to support themselves in areas that were open to the Jews and Conversos.

Cristobal Colon, born into a world of violent anti-Jewish activity to a family of weavers by the name of Colombo, was raised to embrace Christianity. From his writings we know that he carried deep within him the belief that he would follow his namesake, St. Christopher, and carry Christ upon his back across the waters. But by keeping his Genoese background a mystery, he was suspected by scholars of hiding something of potential danger to him and to his family. Had he been born into a Converso family who had fled the 1391 Catalonian massacres, he would have made a conscientious effort to keep his Jewish extraction from the eyes of the Crown and the Church. Thus, Cristoforo Colombo, the son of the master weaver Domenico Colombo, left Genoa at about the age of twenty-two and eventually became the man his contemporaries knew as Cristobal Colon.

2

SHIPWRECKED— PORTUGAL

1476

An example of early sixteenth-century ships from the title page of Pedro de Medina's *Arte de Navegar*, 1545. Reprinted by permission of the British Library.

On August 13, 1476, just off Portugal's southern point of Cape St. Vincent, Cristobal Colon was sailing as a corsair (privateer or sailor of fortune) with a French fleet of twelve caravels outfitted for war. The corsair-admiral, Guillaume de Casenove-Coullon, was the commander of the fleet. A Genoese convoy of five merchant ships carrying mastic (a resin from Mediterranean evergreens used as an astringent) was laboriously making its way north toward Lisbon. Scudding over the waves, Casenove spied the Burgundy flag flying from one of the ships in the Genoese convoy, the *Bechalla*. Since France was at war with Burgundy, Casenove ordered an attack. A fiery battle ensued. At first the well-armed merchant convoy made a gallant attempt to volley shot for shot but they were over-

whelmed by the French. The wooden caravels quickly
caught fire, forcing the Genoese convoy to retreat. They
eventually made port at Cadiz, Spain. With his ship belching
fire and smoke, Colon jumped overboard, grabbed an oar
and washed ashore with shipwrecked French sailors at
Lagos, Portugal, just east of Cape St. Vincent.

This seemingly insignificant sea battle has been pulled
apart and examined by every Columbus scholar because
there are serious doubts as to which side Columbus was
actually on. The Italian advocates firmly place Columbus
with the Genoese convoy while the Spanish scholars claim
that Columbus was a young corsair sailing with Casenove.

The Italian advocates claim that Columbus was on the
ship *Bechalla*, which was manned by seamen from Savona.[1]
While it is known that Columbus was employed by the
Genoese merchants Centurione and Spinola in 1478–1479,
scholars speculate that he was with the Genoese convoy in
1476. They have ascertained from Genoese documents that
Columbus was in both Genoa and Savona in the early 1470s.
The documents specifically note that a Cristoforo Colombo
was in the Genoese courts in September and October of
1470, in Savona in March and August of 1472, and again in
Savona in August of 1473.[2] He was representing his father on
these occasions, often paying his father's debts. The suggestion here is that Domenico Colombo may have been a heavy
drinker and that his wife and children were responsible for
his debts. Scholars go on to suggest that beginning in his late
teens, Columbus found he could earn more money at sea
than at his father's loom. It is most probable that during the
early 1470s Columbus began making short business trips by
sea to Savona in order to sell his father's woven goods and
wine, a side business Domenico had started. It is interesting

to note that when following the coastline, Savona is west of Genoa, close to Catalonia. While we know Columbus frequented Savona, we have no evidence that he was sailing with the men from Savona on the *Bechalla* during the 1476 battle. Even Morison concedes that "his name is not found on the list of officers or passengers, so he must have been a common seaman."[3] But we know from Columbus's own writings that by the age of twenty-one he was not a common seaman as Morison suggests. Columbus had been a corsair since 1472.

Corsairs were an interesting breed of privateers, the need for them arising from constant warfare on the European continent. Most often they were captains who owned their ships and were hired by different countries either to protect merchant convoys or to aggressively hunt them down. Corsairs were also hired to augment a war fleet, and this is what Spanish scholars suspect Columbus was doing in the 1476 battle. In one of Columbus's most revealing letters to King Ferdinand and Queen Isabella, dated January 1495, he wrote that he had been hired as a corsair in 1472 by King Rene d'Anjou. He claimed to have sailed from Savona with orders to attack the Aragonese vessel, *Fernandina*. It is surprising that Columbus would admit this to King Ferdinand since the *Fernandina* was most probably named after him and, at the time, he was engaging in an act of war against Aragon, part of Ferdinand's kingdom. However, it was twenty-three years after the event, and he must have felt secure enough to reveal this information to the king. Columbus wrote:

> It happened to me that king Rene (whom God hath taken) sent me to Tunis to capture the galleass

Fernandina; and being off the island of S. Pietro near
Sardinia I was told there were two ships and a carrack
with the said galleass, which disturbed my people, and
they resolved to go no further, but to sail right back to
Marseilles and pick up another ship and more people. I,
seeing that nothing could be done against the force of
their wills without some stratagem, yielded to their de-
sires, and then "changing the feed" of the needle, made
sail when night fell, and on the following day at sunup
we found ourselves off Cape Carthage while all aboard
were certain we were on our way to Marseilles.[4]

This was the first of many ingenious strategies Columbus
used throughout his voyages to force his men to follow his
commands. He used a similar scheme in faking the distance
traveled on his first historic voyage as well as other chican-
ery to keep himself and his crew alive. One must try to
imagine how hard it must have been for a twenty-one-year-
old captain to convince a crew of tough sailors (perhaps
some of them pirates) to sail into battle against four well-
armed vessels. Only by changing the compass needle was he
able to approach the ship he had been ordered to take. The
Italian advocates never made the connection that since Columbus had been a corsair for the French in 1472, he might
very well have continued in their service, finding himself
under the command of Admiral Casenove-Coullon in 1476.

Further investigation brings more facts to light. While
Columbus was in the service of King Rene d'Anjou, searching for the *Fernandina*, he was fighting against King Ferdinand's father, Juan II of Aragon. Rene d'Anjou was backing
a Catalonian rebellion against the Aragonese, who were
trying to retain control over Catalonia. Clearly, the French

were helping the Catalonians in their effort to extract themselves from Aragon. Keeping in mind that the 1391 riots destroyed most of Aragon's Jewish communities, it may not have been surprising to find Columbus fighting with the French. If indeed a Jewish Colombo family had fled Catalonia during the riots, then Columbus might have had a vested interest in throwing over the Aragonese. He may not have been simply the free-wheeling corsair the Italian advocates suggest he was.

It is possible that Columbus hoped his own family would be able to return to Catalonia if it was no longer dominated by Aragon. Of course we can only speculate here, but these speculations help fill in the mysteries surrounding Columbus's life. The Jewish scholar Kayserling investigated the nautical world of Catalonia in the fourteenth century. He writes, "The Spaniards, particularly the people of Catalonia and Aragon, were especially active in maritime affairs. Their shipping and foreign trade developed so rapidly that they rivalled, and, in fact, soon surpassed, the mercantile marine of Venice, Pisa, and Genoa, the older commercial cities of Italy."[5] But what is even more fascinating is that a number of highly influential Jews were an integral part of this nautical trade. Kayserling (pp. 2, 5, 6) mentions R. Jehudano of Valencia, treasurer of King Jaime I, who organized whole fleets for the king. He also notes that Juceff Faquin of Barcelona was a renowned navigator and that Mestre Jaime, the noted nautical scholar of Prince Henry the Navigator's academy at Sagres, was really Jehuda Cresques of Palma (a city in Catalonia). Cresques was in Catalonia during the 1391 riots, fled to Barcelona, and then took the name of Jaime Ribes. In 1438 he was appointed director of Prince Henry's academy, where he practiced his art of cartography.

His maps were highly sought after, and he was considered the most respected scholar in his field.[6]

It is evident, then, that there was a very rich nautical Jewish heritage predating Columbus. If the Colombo/Colon family did flee Catalonia in 1391, they would have been well acquainted with the powerful Jewish nautical world. Columbus may have been well connected to Jewish merchants living in Catalonia, Savona, and Genoa, merchants who would give a young sailor a fair exchange for his father's goods, making it possible for him to earn his livelihood on the sea.

This suggestion gains more weight when one considers the fact that Columbus claimed not only to have been a corsair at the age of twenty-one but also to have been related to an admiral. No such claim could be taken lightly in the fifteenth century. The admiralty, like other commanding offices, was reserved strictly for the royalty. King Ferdinand's grandfather, Don Fadrique, had been an admiral. How then could a young corsair claim to be related to an admiral? Surely Morison's "common seaman" could not make such a claim. Morison did not try to figure out who this admiral could have been. But what if Columbus had been trying to prove himself to someone, perhaps to an admiral in his family, when he so boldly changed the needle on the compass and doggedly pursued the *Fernandina*? While he never gave the name of his familial admiral, Columbus wrote, "I am not the first Admiral in my family—let them give me the name they will, for, after all, David, a very wise King, kept ewes and later was made a king of Jerusalem, and I am the servant of that same Lord who raised David to that state."[7] Not only did Columbus assert that there had been another admiral in his family, but he also linked this claim with a

Judaic reference to King David. The mystery persists, however; who was the first admiral in the Colombo family?

Research has revealed that the name Coullon (part of the last name of Casenove, which Morison completely omits in his biography), translates into Colombo in Italian and Colon in Spanish. It seems that Admiral Casenove-Coullon might well have been related to Columbus, might well have been the admiral Columbus was referring to in his letter to King Ferdinand. Roth writes that there was a direct connection between the French, Italian, and Spanish Colons. He notes:

> The name "Colon" is met with only, it seems, among persons of French origin. . . . the route of the exiles from France who arrived in Italy is well known. On coming over the Alps, they settled down in Piedmont, where the three communities of Asti, Fossano and Moncalvo followed the old French tradition. It was with this part of Italy, in the hinterland of Genoa, that the Jewish Colon-Colombo family was associated.[8]

Madariaga's work adds more light to this mysterious admiral when he points out that Admiral Casenove-Coullon had been referred to as Admiral Colon by his contemporaries. Madariaga quotes the chronicler Diego de Valera, who wrote, "Of the case which befell the Captain of the French fleet called Colon in the Cape of St. Mary, which is thirty-six leagues from the city of Cadiz. . . ."[9] Madariaga goes on to state that King Ferdinand referred to Casenove-Coullon as Admiral Colon before Columbus ever landed in Spain.[10] So when Columbus wished to be styled a "Don and Admiral of the Ocean Sea," he did, it seems, have a precedent, a right to this claim. Very simply, Columbus may not have been the first Colon to be an admiral. He may have based his right to an admiralty on a probable connection to the famous admiral Casenove-Coullon or Colon.

There is still one more key point suggesting that Columbus was indeed sailing with the French rather than with the Genoese in that fateful battle off Cape St. Vincent. We know that after the battle the Genoese ships retreated to the Cadiz port. Columbus, however, washed ashore in Lagos along with French and Portuguese sailors from the French fleet. What, then, was a Genoese sailor doing with the shipwrecked French fleet? We know that Columbus was the corsair-captain of a French ship in 1472, and it seems likely that he was a corsair under the command of his renowned supposed relative Admiral Casenove-Coullon, fighting for the French against the Genoese merchants in 1476. Let us go back for a moment to the supposition that the Colombo family fled Catalonia, lived in Genoa, but never assimilated because of their Jewish extraction. It is possible, then, to put the facts in order. Columbus, Cristobal Colon, would have felt little allegiance to Genoa and consequently could have fired upon a Genoese convoy. With his ship ablaze, he jumped overboard and fortuitously washed ashore in Portugal, one of the most powerful naval kingdoms of the fifteenth century.

3

PORTUGAL—AN IDEA TAKES HOLD

1476

החכם דון יצחק אברבנאל מאיטאליא,
נקבר בפאדובאה/מ אברבנל טי'דת נפ רם'ה לפ'ק

Portrait of Don Isaac Abravanel, who died in Venice in 1508.

When Columbus was shipwrecked in 1476, Portugal had become one of the most powerful naval kingdoms in all of Europe. In 1385, King Joao I defeated Castile in the battle of Aljubarrota, and reestablished the Portuguese kingdom. From the time King Joao I became grand master of the military order of Aviz, maritime trade became Portugal's life blood. Trading with England and Flanders, Joao was able to export grain, salt, olive oil, wine, honey, cork, leather, and broomstraw. While Joao was busy consolidating his power, the Black Death swept through Portugal, killing one out of every three people. Joao used this catastrophe to his advantage by confiscating all unclaimed lands. These new lands gave additional strength to the Crown, resulting in a weaker feudal system of dukes, counts, and other petty rulers. The consolidation of power gave Joao additional access to funds that he used toward maritime exploration. Of Joao's five sons, the two most famous were Duarte, who followed as Joao's heir, ruling from 1433 to 1438, and Prince Henry, better known as Henry the Navigator.

Under King Duarte's short five-year rule, Prince Henry established an institute devoted to maritime studies in Sagres. As previously noted, Henry encouraged scholars such as Mestre Jaime Ribes (Cresques) to live, study, and teach at this institute. With a twofold quest in mind, and with backing from his brother, Prince Henry financed explorations of the African coast as early as 1434. Henry's first goal was to find Prester John, a priest who, according to legend, had discovered a fabulous land of precious gems, pearls, and gold. The legends claimed that Prester John had discovered the fountain of youth, as well as stones that could heal the blind eye. Some of the Prester John legends claimed that his kingdom was in the heart of Africa, while others claimed that it was somewhere near the land of the Grand Khan (China). Many of the early discoverers were certain they were close to finding Prester John. Even Columbus searched for him when he was exploring Cuba.

Prince Henry's second quest was to find an ocean route to India as well as to Cipango (Japan) and the land of the Grand Khan. Though some historians claim that the fall of Constantinople to the Turks in 1453 was the catalyst for the age of discovery, Prince Henry had already been exploring the African coast for more than twenty years. By 1434 Henry's caravels had rounded the African Cape Bajador, and Captain Antao Goncalves Baldaia had reached the Tropic of Cancer.

King Duarte died in 1438. He left the regency for his young son, King Afonso V, to his consort, Queen Leonore, and to his bastard brother, the count of Barcelos. However, Don Pedro, King Duarte's younger brother, contested the regency, and won his case in the Portuguese courts. Queen Leonore left Portugal to seek help from her brother, Juan II of Aragon (King Ferdinand's father), but she never returned. There were rumors that Don Pedro had ordered Leonore's death.

Don Pedro enforced a rigid anti-baronial policy, undermining the lesser noblemen. In 1442, the count of Barcelos was granted the dukedom of Braganza, and his influence over the young King Afonso grew. The duke of Braganza, along with other noblemen, plotted Don Pedro's downfall. The duke revealed to the king what had been rumored at the time of his mother's death—that Don Pedro had arranged her murder. In 1449 the enraged young king gathered a small army at the Douro River where he confronted his uncle, Don Pedro. Within minutes Don Pedro fell in battle. As a result, the duke of Braganza now took Don Pedro's place as the king's most trusted man and became one of the most powerful men in Portugal. With the duke of Braganza's rise to power, so too rose a Jewish family who served as a direct link between the Jewish community and the royal house, the Abravanels.

* * *

Life for the Jews of Portugal had become severely restricted under Don Pedro's anti-Jewish laws called *The Ordinances*. Each year the laws grew more stringent, making life for the Jews of Portugal very difficult. Jews had to be within the walls of the Juderias by the tolling of sunset bells and could not leave until the gates were opened in the morning. They could not leave the Juderias without wearing a yellow badge. They paid enormous taxes for the right to practice their religion. These laws dictated their lives from the size of their buildings to the number of ribbons and rings they could wear. They could not bear arms and most guilds were closed to them. Their very survival was determined by the whim of Don Pedro. However, with his death and the subsequent rise in power of the duke of Braganza, life for the Portuguese Jews dramatically changed. The duke introduced the Jewish treasurer, Don Judah Abravanel, to the court and helped Don Judah and his son Isaac become indispensable to King Afonso. With the Abravanels at court, the Jews finally had influential men to represent them, and the anti-Jewish policies of Don Pedro were no longer enforced.

In the service of kings for at least three generations, the Abravanels were well acquainted with the political intrigues of kings and constantly worked for the welfare of the Jews. After the 1391 riots that raged throughout all the Spains, the Converso Juan Sanchez de Sevilla, treasurer to King Enrique III of Castile, decided to return to his Judaism, resuming his Jewish name, Samuel Abravanel. He could no longer live with the hypocrisy of ostensibly being a Catholic while in his heart he still cherished the Jewish faith of his forefathers. Samuel Abravanel fled to Portugal, for if he had stayed in Spain, he would have been tried by the Church as a heretic. Relapsing to Judaism was a crime that carried the death sentence. In Portugal Samuel Abravanel quickly rose to become the treasurer for the youngest son of Joao I, Don Fernando, but when the young Fernando died in Tangiers, Abravanel was called into the service of the bastard prince, the count of Barcelos (who was to become the duke of Braganza). Samuel Abravanel's son, Judah, also served the count/duke of Braganza and, as stated, rose in power along with the duke.

By 1476, the year Columbus was washed ashore, Don Judah Abravanel's son, Isaac, was already well entrenched as royal treasurer to the duke of Braganza, and was closest friends with the duke's grandson, Don Fernando. By this time, Isaac Abravanel was also the trusted treasurer of King Afonso V. It is not known for certain that Columbus met Isaac Abravanel in Portugal, but it is known that Abravanel was instrumental in helping Columbus with his enterprise in Spain. It certainly is possible that their friendship extended back to the 1470s in Portugal.

When Columbus arrived in Lisbon in 1476, Jewish cartographers and astronomers were enjoying great prestige at Prince Henry's academy in Sagres. Caravels were returning from Africa with slaves and gold from trading posts that had been established by Henry in the 1460s. The most noted Jews at Sagres, besides Mestre Jaime, were Mestre Joseph Vizinho and the renowned Spanish-Jewish scholar, Abraham Zacuto.

In 1470, King Afonso's son, Prince Joao, was made the king's First Lord of the Admiralty and Secretary of State for the Colonies.[1] Like his great-uncle, Prince Henry, Joao was determined to find a route to India by rounding Africa. In 1474 he wrote to the most famous cosmographer of the time, Paolo del Pozzo Toscanelli, concerning such a route. Toscanelli answered the prince on June 25, 1474 (two years before Columbus arrived). In his letter he wrote:

> . . . a map made by my own hands, from which you should begin to make the journey ever towards the West, and the places which you should reach and how far from the Pole or from the equinoctial line you ought to turn, and how many leagues you will have to cross to

reach those regions most fertile in all kinds of spices and jewels and precious stones; and think it not marvellous that I call West the land of spices, while it is usually said that spices come from the East, for whoever navigates Westward in the lower hemisphere shall always find the said paths West and whoever travels Eastward by land in the higher hemisphere shall always find the same land East.[2]

This letter was in Joao's hands well before he had ever heard of Christopher Columbus. Joao knew that Toscanelli felt the East could be reached by sailing west. While this letter was kept secret and vaulted after Joao received it, the general idea that one could reach the East by sailing west must have slipped from the lips of those who had seen it. By the time Columbus arrived in Lisbon the secret must have been out, but only Columbus devoted his life to finding that route.

Fortuitously, when Columbus was shipwrecked and washed ashore in Lagos, his brother Bartholomew was living in Lisbon and working as a cartographer. Columbus joined him in Lisbon and for a short time the brothers worked together. This leads to the next set of mysteries surrounding Columbus; all his surviving documents are written in Castilian and Latin, not in Italian. Where and when did he learn his written languages?

Columbus's few scribbled notes in Italian were poorly written, and show that he did not have writing facility in that language. The letters he wrote to the San Georgio Bank in Genoa, years later, were not in Italian. He did not attend school in Genoa, for his name does not appear on any of the lists which, amazingly, still exist. The Italian advocates disagree with the Spanish over how Columbus acquired his ability to write in Castilian and Latin. The Italian advocates note that there was an active Genoese community in Lisbon when Columbus arrived, and they suggest that Columbus learned his Castilian and Latin in that community.

The Spanish advocates make a far different case. They believe that being of Catalonian descent, Columbus acquired his Castilian in his Spanish-Jewish home. A contemporary of Columbus and one of his biographers, Las Casas, gave some information concerning this curious fact that Columbus communicated in Castilian and Latin rather than in Italian. Las Casas claimed that Columbus spoke Castilian with some difficulty, writing, "He seems to be a native of another language, for he does not fully grasp the meaning of the words of the Castilian language nor of its way of speaking."[3] The Spanish advocates put forth the suggestion that Columbus was speaking a fourteenth-century Castilian, dating back to the time his family fled Catalonia, and that this was slightly different from Las Casas' fifteenth-century Castilian. Madariaga notes that "his language was not the Spanish of the fifteenth century, but that of the fourteenth; it had remained unevolved in that lopped-off branch transplanted to Genoa towards 1390, and had undoubtedly absorbed many Italianisms."[4] When the Spanish Jews fled Spain in 1391 and again in 1492 at the time of the Expulsion, they continued to speak their form of Castilian while the Spanish language continued to evolve. The Jewish Castilian remained relatively unchanged from the way it had been spoken at the time they had fled. A form of this language still exists today called Ladino, a form of old Castilian. It is possible that even though Castilian was Columbus's first language, he may have had trouble being understood when he spoke his Castilian in Spain.

A second argument supporting the hypothesis that Columbus's first language was Castilian is the fact that Columbus's notes in the margins of his books were written in Castilian and Latin. These notes were written before Columbus arrived in Spain. Columbus had a copy of *Imago Mundi* written by Cardinal d'Ailly of Germany, in which he discusses how much of the world is habitable. In his copy of d'Ailly, he wrote notes concerning the prophet Esdras's (Ezra's) apocryphal writings. Columbus wrote notes in the margins of his copy of Pope Pius II's *Historia rerum ubique gestarum* (A History of Events). His copy of *The Book of Ser Marco Polo* was also marked up. All of these notes were written in Castilian and Latin. Roth comments that "even when he communicated with the Bank of St. George in Genoa, he used Spanish. What is more, he spoke and wrote in Spanish before he came to Spain, for marginal notes from his hand, clearly dated 1481, are in that language."[5]

Columbus's mistakes in his use of Latin provide additional grounds for speculation over his extraction. Morison claims that Columbus's Latin grammatical structure showed that he was thinking in Portuguese. This suggests that Castilian was not his first language and that he was not of Spanish descent. However, Roth states that Columbus's mistakes were Spanish in nature. He notes that "when this Genoese weaver's son attempted to write in Latin, which he so often did, his errors betray the fact that he was thinking in Spanish, for they are precisely those which a Spaniard might be expected to make."[6] None of the scholars suggests that the grammatical mistakes were made by someone thinking in Italian. The simple question remains: if his mother tongue was Italian, why wasn't he thinking in Italian? It seems, once again, that the Spanish advocates are more on target.

Though Columbus's Spanish was different from the Spanish spoken in the late fifteenth century, he certainly seemed to have been thinking in Spanish well before he arrived in Spain. Once again the mysteries fade when one considers Columbus to have been from a Spanish-speaking Catalonian family living in Genoa. We may never know, however, if it was luck or careful planning that brought the Columbus brothers to Portugal, land of the discoverers.

4

REACHING THE EAST BY SAILING WEST

1477

Columbus with an astrolabe, from André Thevet's *Portraits et Vies des Hommes Illustres*. Reprinted by permission of the British Library.

By 1477 Columbus was working with his brother Bartholomew in a Lisbon chart shop, learning the art of cartography. The active Lisbon port was bustling with ships from Scandinavia, England, Flanders, the Spains, Genoa, and the North African coast. Each day the smells of the sea, the pitch and tar, the salty air must have beckoned him, for by now sailing must have been in his blood. He would have seen the African slaves, the gold dust, Malagueta pepper, and elephant tusks. The slaves, along with the goods, would be sold and traded for horses, Venetian glass beads, red caps, and hawks' bells. Not only would Columbus have been surrounded by the sights and smells of the sea but he would have been at the very hub of talk and speculation about finding a route to the Indies by sailing around Africa.

Indeed, every year more progress was made in defining the coast of Africa. In 1456 Prince Henry had been granted papal permission to explore and lay claim to the Gold and Ivory Coasts, giving Portugal a virtual commercial monopoly in Africa. By 1469, King Afonso V had granted Fernao Gomes the right to explore one hundred leagues each year. By 1474, Gomes had reached Fernando Po, the point where the continent turns south.[1]

It seems that the call of the sea and the excitement of exploration proved too much for Columbus to stay cooped up in his brother's shop. We know that during this period he sailed south to Africa and then made at least one trip to England and further north. Much later, on his voyages to the New World, he made several references to these early trips, comparing the flora and fauna in the New World to what he had seen in Africa and north of England. On these early sea voyages he was slowly, carefully, methodically collecting evidence to support his idea that one could reach the East by sailing west.

His most important fact-finding voyage was to Iceland. There he came across two curiosities that lent credence to his fantastic idea, an idea that probably took hold after hearing part or all of Toscanelli's words. First, he noted that people lived in the "torrid zone," a zone that Ptolemy had thought to be uninhabitable. Second, he noted that Ptolemy had underestimated the amount of land on the earth's surface.

* * *

Ptolemy had lived in Alexandria between 100–170 A.D. and had written *Almagest* or *Geographical Outline*, which became the standard for all geographic navigation until Columbus and other great explorers began to prove him wrong. Ptolemy believed that the earth was at the center of the universe and that the sun, moon, planets, and stars circled around it. This work was not just the standard for geographers but had become the way most educated men perceived the world, and had become part of Church doctrine. It was not until the late 1400s that Copernicus put forward his theories, which would change the Ptolemaic perception of the world forever. Though Columbus suspected Ptolemy's mathematics to be incorrect, Ptolemy was, in fact, more accurate than Columbus. Greatly influenced by Marco Polo, Columbus guessed that Cipango (Japan) and Cathay (China) were much closer to the European continent than they actually are.

On this voyage to Tile (Iceland), Columbus made his first remarks concerning Ptolemy, and they indicate that he was already gathering information to support his plan. Columbus wrote:

> I sailed in the year 1477, in the month of February, a hundred leagues beyond the island of Tile, whose northern part is in latitude 73°N and not 63° as some would have it be; nor does it lie on the meridian where Ptolemy says the west begins, but much further west.[2]

Not only did Columbus note the first of Ptolemy's inaccuracies, but he also saw two Asian-looking people who had clung to driftwood and washed ashore in Iceland. Their broad faces convinced the twenty-six-year-old Columbus that they had originated from the East (most probably they had drifted from Finland). In the margin of his copy of

Historia Rerum, he made the observation, "Men of Cathay which is toward the Orient have come hither. We have seen many remarkable things, especially in Gallway of Ireland, a man and a woman of extraordinary appearance in two boats adrift."[3] These observations helped confirm his incorrect guess that Asia was significantly closer than Ptolemy and other noted scholars had estimated.

We know of one other voyage in 1478 that Columbus made for the Genoese merchant Ludavico Centurione. He was hired by Centurione's Lisbon partner Paolo Di Negro to transport sugar from Lisbon to Madeira. Di Negro had given Columbus an insufficient amount of ducats to buy the sugar, and Columbus had to appear in the Genoese courts in August 1479 concerning this transaction. Madariaga (p. 82) notes that the Negro family in Lisbon was a well-known, powerful Jewish family. No one, however, has been able to identify Paolo Di Negro as part of that family, but it is possible that Columbus was sailing for this powerful Portuguese Jewish family.

During the same year of 1479, Columbus was back in Lisbon where he frequented the chapel of the Convento dos Santos, a convent for the daughters of wealthy noblemen. By visiting this convent he must have hoped to attract a nobleman's pretty daughter. This was one of the very few ways in which a young man of no means would have had access to the aristocracy. He met the 25-year-old Dona Felipa Perestrello e Moniz, who, at this age must have been overlooked by other suitors. Though she was of noble birth, the family was far from wealthy.

Don Bartholomew Perestrello, Felipa's father, was a nobleman who had fought with Prince Henry in an African Crusade. Perestrello had been granted the right to help colonize the Madeira Island of Porto Santo with two other men. He had taken a pregnant rabbit on the first coloniz- ing expedition in hopes of raising game. The rabbit gave birth, and then she and her brood proceeded to multiply so rapidly that the island was soon overrun with rabbits that ended up destroying all the green vegetation. Needless to say, this was a demoralizing adventure as well as a finan- cial disaster. Don Bartholomew made a second attempt to colonize Porto Santo but still the rabbits destroyed any vegetation that the settlers tried to grow. Eventually Peres- trello returned to Lisbon and died in 1457. He did, however, leave behind a number of charts concerning the trade winds of Porto Santo, in which Columbus took great interest. Dona Felipa offered exactly what Columbus needed, a wife who was descended from nobility. Her brother, Barthol- omew II, was captain and governor of Porto Santo and was gaining an upper hand over the rabbits. Columbus must have realized all the tremendous advantages he'd have with this marriage. Not only was he marrying into the Portuguese nobility, but he could live on the Madeira Islands just off Morocco, where the ships embarking on their voyages of discovery passed before heading down Africa's coast. Co- lumbus married Dona Felipa and moved to Porto Santo. Their son, Diego, was born there in late 1479 or early 1480. On Porto Santo, Columbus carefully mapped the trade winds of the islands. This information would eventually lead to his extraordinary success.

Columbus had done very well for himself. The young shipwrecked corsair had married into the nobility and had set himself up directly on the route to Africa. During this period he made at least one voyage to St. George of the Mine, a Portuguese fortification on the African Gold Coast in

Guinea. On this voyage he gathered more proof that the scholars were wrong. Columbus noted, "It is not uninhabitable, for the Portuguese sail through it today, and it is even very populous, and under the equator is the castle of Mina of the most serene king of Portugal, which we have seen."[4] Columbus was beginning to realize that the land mass of the earth was much greater and much more populated than had been previously calculated. He realized that his own observations concurred with Marco Polo's writings.

On constant alert for more conclusive information concerning land on the other side of the western ocean, Columbus collected interesting bits of information from sailors living on the Madeira Islands. Martin Vincent told him about a carved piece of wood that had floated in from the west. Columbus's brother-in-law, Pero Correa, had also seen carved wood that had drifted in. Columbus also made note of two people who had been discovered in the Azores, "who seemed to have wide faces and of a different shape from the Christians."[5] Carefully collecting his facts, he put together his own theory that the earth was far more habitable than previous scholars had suggested, and that the land masses were much greater, therefore much closer than previously estimated.

Columbus also continued to pore over his father-in-law's charts, and drew new ones. He became extremely knowledgeable concerning the islands' trade winds. Madariaga points out that

Columbus had equipped himself with the best and most scientific information on winds, currents and general navigating conditions west of the Madeira group of islands. In short, subsequent events proved him to be so skilful [sic] a navigator and so excellent an Atlantic pilot, that a wide sailing experience at this time and in these seas becomes of necessity an indispensable part of his life-story.[6]

One can well imagine a young Columbus, the proud father of a son whose noble connections hailed back to the time of Joao I, standing on a promontory, noting the trade winds and piecing together his ideas. It all must have seemed well within his grasp. All he had to do was convince the king.

Approaching the king was no simple task, even for someone with noble connections, because King Afonso of Portugal was fighting in Spain. King Afonso's sister, Juana, had married Enrique IV of Castile, but it was rumored that Enrique was impotent. When Queen Juana had a child, the Infanta Juana, the people were so convinced that the child's father was the knight Beltran de la Cueva, that the Infanta was nicknamed La Beltranaja. When King Enrique died in 1474, King Afonso of Portugal married his niece the Infanta, La Beltranaja, hoping to wrest the crown away from Isabella and Ferdinand. King Afonso was soundly defeated by the young Ferdinand and, despairing after the defeat, Afonso went off on a pilgrimage to the Holy Land. During his absence, Joao II ruled but finally, King Afonso returned to Portugal, a brokenhearted old man. It was not until King Afonso's death in 1481, that Joao II (King John II) ascended the Portuguese throne.

The fate of Columbus as well as the fate of the Jews swung with the death of King Afonso. Afonso had been the Jews' protector and had counted heavily upon Don Isaac Abravanel to raise funds for his ill-fated Spanish-Portuguese

War. Don Isaac served the king well and also remained extremely close to his dear friend Fernando, who was now the duke of Braganza. King Joao was certain that his cousins, the duke of Braganza and the duke of Viseu, were plotting to overthrow him and seize the crown. Joao was prepared to go to any lengths to eliminate his enemies (real or imagined), to subjugate the wealthy nobility, and to consolidate his power. He accused the duke of Braganza of corresponding with King Ferdinand in Castile, and arrested him for high treason. Don Isaac, guilty only by association, fled Portugal to Spain in 1483. From there, Abravanel wrote to King Joao, asserting his innocence. The king permitted Don Isaac's family to join him in Spain. Sadly, the duke of Braganza, a great friend and patron of the Jews, was beheaded. King Joao stabbed the duke of Viseu in the back when he had come to pledge his allegiance. Thus, the nobility was quickly and ruthlessly subdued. Many of the anti-Jewish laws, the *Ordinances*, created under Don Pedro's regency for the young king Afonso, were reinstated.

In 1484, Columbus was finally granted an audience with King Joao. It is easy to imagine Columbus preparing for his audience with the ruthless king. With maps and calculations in hand, now a member of the proud nobility, most probably dressed in velvet and satin, Columbus strode into the throneroom. It was recorded that he was a tall redhead, with shining blue eyes. He must have cut a dashing figure but still he had to convince Mestre Joseph Vizinho, Mestre Rodrigo, and Diogo Ortiz de Vilhegas, all members of the Maritime Advisory Committee, that it was possible to sail the Western Sea to reach the land of the Grand Khan.

Mestre Joseph Vizinho and Mestre Rodrigo, who were always consulted in matters of astronomy and mathematics, were Jews. Joseph Vizinho had been a pupil of Abraham Zacuto, a renowned scholar whose work Columbus also studied. Zacuto taught in Salamanca, Spain, and had published an astronomical work called *Ha-Hibbur ha-Gadol*. Zacuto wrote about the stars and eclipses and had invented a superior astrolabe that gave sailors precise sun positions, helping them ascertain latitude with greater accuracy. Columbus relied upon Zacuto's eclipse predictions, which saved him and his crew on his fourth voyage.

Columbus unfurled his maps and presented his proposal. He claimed that the mathematics previously calculated by men like Ptolemy was inaccurate and discussed the fact that men were living in places Ptolemy had claimed uninhabitable. The mathematics he presented was based on the work of the Moslem geographer Alfragan, but Columbus had shortened Alfragan's degree by using the measurement for a Roman mile rather than for an Arabic mile. His final estimate for the circumference of the globe was off by 75 percent. Columbus also had stretched the length of Asia, according to Marco Polo's report, and had come up with a measurement of Europe and "The Indies" at 283°, calculating that he only had 68° of ocean to cross.[7] It did not take the committee very long to assess Columbus's gross underestimate compared to all other estimates. Many years later, in 1552, Joao de Barros mentions in his *Decades of Asia* Columbus's interview with King Joao and the Maritime Advisory Committee. Barros wrote:

> The king, as he observed this Christovão Colom to be a big talker and boastful in setting forth his accomplishments, and full of fancy and imagination with his Isle

Cypango than certain whereof he spoke, gave him small credit. However, by strength of his importunity it was ordered that he confer with D. Diogo Ortiz bishop of Ceuta and Master Rodrigo and Master José, to whom the king had committed these matters of cosmography and discovery, and they all considered the words of Christovão Colom as vain, simply founded on imagination, or things like the Isle Cypango of Marco Polo.[8]

Diogo Ortiz de Vilhegas, the head of the committee, was aware of Toscanelli's letter, which strongly suggested that a western crossing of the sea could be made. But even Toscanelli figured the distance from the Canaries to Cipango at 3,000 nautical miles, whereas Columbus calculated 2,400 nautical miles. The actual miles are 10,600.[9]

The other important major obstacle was money. Very simply, Columbus had to be financed. Shortly after Columbus was rejected, King Joao gave his permission to Fernao Dulmo and Joao Estreito to try the expedition because they could finance it themselves. Joao must have been sufficiently impressed with Columbus's proposal to want to give the idea a try. Dulmo and Estreito, however, did not have Columbus's knowledge of the trade winds. They departed from an island in the Azores, and their light caravels could not fight the western winds.[10]

Columbus blamed his rejection on "the Jews" in Joao's court, his anger directed at Vizinho and Rodrigo. It would be the Jews, however, who would ultimately turn his dream into a reality.

5

THE PROGRESSIVE RECONQUISTA

711–1486

Portrait of Queen Isabella of
Castile, attributed to Bartolome
Bermejo, c. 1490. Reprinted by
permission of the British Library.

Portrait of King Ferdinand V of
Aragon from Aliprando
Capriolo's *Ritratti di Cento
Capitani Illustri*, 1596. Reprinted
by permission of the British Library.

With five-year-old Diego, Columbus arrived in Palos, Spain, in 1484. Palos was a small but lively port. Columbus made his way past open-air markets of fish, fruit, vegetables, and baked goods before walking the dusty road to the monastery, La Rabida. Tired and hungry, he and little Diego were received kindly by Fray Juan Perez, who gave them a cool drink of water and some crusty bread. Columbus began a conversation with the friar and spoke of his dream to sail the western sea. Fray Juan was duly impressed and introduced him to Fray Antonio de Marchena, who also quickly realized the merit of Columbus's proposal. They agreed to take in little Diego, and also gave Columbus letters of introduction to two powerful dukes.

What brought Columbus to Spain? Dona Felipa had died, and after Joao's rejection, there was little to keep him in Portugal. The Columbus brothers must have decided to try to obtain audiences with the Spanish and French royal courts. Columbus may have decided to try Spain because that was where Dona Felipa's two sisters lived, and he may have intended to leave Diego in their care. One sister was married to Pero Correa, the other to Miguel de Mulyart. Columbus's facility with Castilian also may have influenced his decision to travel to Spain.

With the friars' letters in hand, Columbus proceeded directly to Don Enrique de Guzman, duke of Medina-Sidonia. The duke was not impressed with the proposal. However the second duke, Don Luis de la Cerda, duke of Medinaceli, was so taken with Columbus's proposal that he was his patron from 1484 until he was finally able to help him obtain a royal audience in 1486.

Why would it have taken a powerful duke two years to arrange such an audience? It seems that Columbus could not have arrived in Spain at a more critical time in its history. In 1484 the Catholic Monarchs were embroiled in their crusade to oust the Moors from Granada, and they had no time to discuss sea explorations. Just prior to Columbus's arrival, the Moors had defeated the Christian army in Axarquis. But the defeat only served to strengthen Ferdinand's and Isabella's resolve to reconquer all the lands that had been the Spains prior to the Moorish conquest in 711.

The Jews had been in Spain long before 711, probably arriving during the time of King Solomon, and thriving there for well over a thousand years. Up until the time Djabal at-Tarik (Gibraltar is a derivation of his name) invaded with his

Moorish army, the Jews had been living under tyrannical Visigothic kings. Each king had a different Jewish policy, some forcing wholesale conversions while others were very patronizing. In 613 King Sisebut expelled the Jews, while the next king, Swintila, revoked the edict. So it went back and forth until 709 when King Witiza, who had patronized the Jews, died, and King Roderick countered the previous protective policy with such harsh restrictions that the Jews were not allowed to trade with Christians. King Roderick died trying to stop Tarik's advance. The Jews openly sided with the Moors, hoping that religious tolerance would come with the conquering armies.[1]

A second Moorish invasion occurred under Mughith ar-Rumi, who made his way north and then laid siege outside the city walls of Cordova. Legends say that on one dark night during the siege, the Jews within Cordova opened the gates for Mughith, and enthusiastically joined forces with his army. It is said that from Cordova across all the Spanish kingdoms, the Jews repeated the act of opening the gates for Moors.

In a third invasion, Musa b. Nusair, who ruled all of North Africa, crossed the straits of Gibraltar in 712. His army crushed the Christian forces as far north as Seville. When he took possession of that city, he ordered the Jews to stand guard. Nusair and Tarik continued to drive their armies north to Toledo but then advanced no further. The new Moorish governors allowed the Jews their religious freedom but levied heavy taxes against both Jews and Christians. The Jews were allowed to have their own judicial courts. They were tax farmers, physicians, and craftsmen. Generally this period has been considered a great renaissance in Jewish history.

The Golden Age is the name given to this flourishing period for the Jews of Spain. Toledo's Jewish community was already well established, so it was no wonder that it became a great Jewish center of learning. Some scholars suggest that the name Toledo has a Jewish derivation. Madariaga notes, "Jewish tradition goes back as far as the days of Solomon for the first settlement of the Jews in Spain, and even credits them with the founding of Toledo, the name of which has been considered by some rabbis as a form of the Hebrew word *Tholedoth*, meaning *generations*."[2] Nestled within the steep slopes of Toledo, there still exist two synagogues that were built during this period. One synagogue, which had been a church called Santa Maria Blanca, has graceful mudejar architecture faded like white lace. Its magnificent white marble pillars, with grand circular arches rising from intricately carved braces, stand in soft shafts of light, a silent tribute to the greatness that epitomized Spanish Jewry. The most exquisite synagogue to be built in this era sits unpretentiously in a rather low building called El Transito, the Great Synagogue. Once inside, however, an awesome testament to what had been the grandeur of the Jews of Spain can still be seen. The lofty cedar ceiling was not destroyed by the hundreds of years of abuse the sanctuary suffered. Though some of the Hebrew letters have crumbled, one can still read the psalms of David in gold letters circling the perimeter of the sanctuary. Brilliant colors of peacock blue, orange, red, and sea green, though softened with age, still grace what had been the mudejar balcony for women. On the left and right of where the Ark was displayed are the fading royal crests of the castle and the lion. Today, if one stands in quiet solitude, it seems possible to conjure the past, to imagine the men in their long black velvet robes, chanting from the Torah, and to picture the women, gazing down as sacred words surrounded them.

These synagogues, along with a few gravestones and street names, are almost all that is left of what had been the highly sophisticated Jewish world. Some of the most important Jewish literature and scholarly work flowered during the Moorish period from 711 until Granada's fall in 1492.

In the eleventh century, the great Jewish poets of Spain began to give expression to the Jews of the Diaspora. Solomon Ibn Gabirol wrote plaintive, provocative poems such as the following.

> Return, O my soul, to God
> Return and refresh thy heart
> Make supplication to Him
> And let thy tears also well up before Him
> Perchance He will command that thou be sent
> From the pit wherein thou liest
> Among boorish men
> Whom thou dost hate and despise.[3]

Judah HaLevi, in the twelfth century, also gave voice to the Jews who still mourned the destruction of the Temple and yearned for a return to Jerusalem.

> My heart is in the east, and I in the uttermost west—
> How can I find savour in food?
> How shall it be sweet to me?
> How shall I render my vows and my bonds,
> While yet Zion lieth beneath the fetter of Edom, and I in Arab
>   chains?

A light thing would it seem to me to leave all the good things
  of Spain—
Seeing how precious in mine eyes to behold the dust of the
  desolate sanctuary.[4]

Perhaps the greatest scholar who was born in Spain was
Moses ben Maimon (Maimonides), who lived from 1135–
1204. His work, *Guide to the Perplexed*, became one of the
most celebrated, and disputed, works within the Jewish religion.
Maimonides reduced many of the complex works of the
ancient rabbis into understandable layman's terms. He in-
corporated an Aristotelian philosophy of an ordered world
into Judaism.

The Moorish reign was not destined to last forever, and
by 1063, the Christian King Sancho Ramirez of Aragon
began the slow, tortuous reconquista. In 1072 King Alfonso
VI of Leon raised troops to add momentum to the reconquista, which would wage for the next four hundred years.
The Christian kings trusted their Jewish subjects more than
they did the Moslems, so that when they recaptured a city
they allowed the Jews to continue as tax collectors, craftsmen, scholars, and physicians. During this turbulent but
romantic period of Spanish history the famous Rodrigo Diaz
de Vivar, better known as El Cid, fought valiantly to retake
Saragossa. El Cid was banished from Castile by King Alfonso, however, for siding with the Moors. After a long siege
that brought about famine and sickness inside the city of
Toledo, King Alfonso finally recaptured the city in 1085. Even
though the Jews loyally served both Moslem and Christian
kings for seven hundred years after the Moorish invasion,
Christians still harbored feelings of distrust.

The most significant movement in the reconquista occurred with the royal marriage of Ferdinand and Isabella in
1469. With this union the petty kingdoms of Aragon, Leon,
and Castile were united in a loose but functional coalition.
Rabbi Abraham Seneor, Isabella's chief tax collector, was
instrumental in arranging the royal marriage. This marriage
arrangement was no simple task, for King Enrique IV,
Isabella's half-brother, was vehemently against it, ordering Ferdinand's arrest should he cross into Castile. Enrique
had declared Isabella his heir only one year before, because
of the pressure concerning the birthright of the Infanta
Juana, La Beltranaja. Enrique hoped to marry Isabella to
King Afonso V of Portugal and thus discreetly be rid of her.
Once he had accomplished that marriage, he would be free
to name the Infanta Juana as his heir. Isabella, however,
had the backing of the Archbishop of Toledo and the noblemen of Castile. Very carefully and secretly, the details for
the young royals were worked out by Abraham Seneor,
Guiterre Cardenas and Alonso de Cabrera between Castile
and Aragon. As a token of his promise to wed, Prince
Ferdinand sent a pearl and ruby necklace to the young
Isabella, who had more need of her warrior prince than
a necklace. However, at that moment, the seventeen-
year-old Ferdinand was proving himself a valiant warrior
in Roussillon. They finally celebrated their marriage on
October 18, 1469 in Juan de Vivero's palace with 2,000
guests in attendance. One can well imagine the magnifi-
cently dressed guests as the nobility came to pledge its
support to the young couple. The women were dressed in
soft velvets and silk brocades, with pearls and precious
stones strung in their hair and around their necks. The
men, with silver, gem-studded swords, wore golden rings

on their fingers, and gold chains hanging heavily around their necks.

* * *

It is important to understand Isabella at this critical time in her life. While she was prepared to dress in the full array of a queen, she was basically a modest, rigid, fanatically religious woman. A strict believer in the divine right to rule, she was certain that the monarchy was a God-given right. She was uneasy about ascending the throne until she was certain that the Infanta Juana was not King Enrique's child. She firmly believed that once she was crowned queen, her decisions would be, in fact, the will of God, and that she would be rewarded with military victories. The Archbishop of Toledo crowned her after the death of King Enrique, but it was not until Beltran de la Cueva bowed to her, pledging his loyalty (implying that the Infanta Juana was his child and not the king's) that she was convinced she had the divine right to rule. When King Afonso V of Portugal committed the unthinkable act of marrying his niece, the Beltranaja, he started the Spanish-Portuguese war. This war proved a testing ground for the Catholic Monarchs' ability to fight. Two important things were accomplished with the defeat of the Portuguese. First, King Afonso was defeated so decisively that he never again proved to be a threat. Second, the Catholic Monarchs showed that with the consolidation of power between Castile, Leon, and Aragon, they were a force to be reckoned with, a real threat to the Moslems who were still in the Spains. The Catholic Monarchs were ready, at last, to pursue the quest of their forefathers, the reconquista, begun so long ago by King Ramirez and King Alfonso in the eleventh century.

During this period, the Catholic Monarchs were surrounded by influential Jews and converted Jews. In the same year Columbus arrived, 1484, Don Isaac Abravanel had been introduced to Isabella through Abraham Seneor and had been working as a royal tax collector. But the Jews and Conversos were already in serious jeopardy throughout the Spains. Ferdinand had expelled the Jews from Andalusia in 1483, and as the scholar Netanyahu states, plans for the complete expulsion of the Jews were already under consideration. Netanyahu writes:

> It is more than probable that Ferdinand's plan for the total expulsion of the Jews was conceived already in 1483, when he ordered their expulsion from Andalusia. But in 1483 it was not in his interest to stamp himself, in the eyes of the Jews, as radically anti-Jewish. Then, and years thereafter, he was still badly in need of Jewish experience and ability, especially in the field of taxation.[5]

Exiled from Portugal, Abravanel mourned the death of his beloved friend, Fernando, the duke of Braganza. He was not eager to return to the service of kings but took refuge in his studies, working on commentaries of the biblical books Joshua and Judges. Abravanel felt that his worldly misfortunes had occurred because he had spent too much time with political intrigues, rather than devoting himself to his religious work. But when Abraham Seneor implored him to bring his vast financial experience to the Spanish court and serve the Catholic Monarchs, he could not refuse. He knew better than most how critical it was for the Jews to have representatives within the royal circle. Though Abravanel was well aware that the Jews were in a tenuous position with the rise of the Catholic Monarchs, he did not, it seems, fully grasp how very treacherous the Crown and the Church could be.

By 1486, the Spanish Inquisition was in full operation. Fray Tomas Torquemada, Isabella's childhood confessor, had already been appointed Grand Inquisitor, and heretics were dying in autos de fé. Ferdinand and Isabella were extending the Inquisition to Aragon, and though the Aragonese court tried to fight it, they were not strong enough to stop its expansion. It seems then, that when Columbus finally arrived at the Spanish Royal Court, he was indeed walking a fine line between pushing for his expedition and keeping his origins shrouded in mystery.

6

COLUMBUS AND THE CONVERSOS AT COURT

1486–1487

A prisoner being examined by Inquisitors.

In April 1486, Columbus was granted his first audience with Ferdinand and Isabella. As he walked into the royal Alcazar in Cordova, he must have felt great trepidation. King Joao II had thought little of his proposal and finally, now, after two years of waiting in Spain, his chance to present his proposal to the Catholic Monarchs was at hand. The Franciscan friars had been duly impressed with his ideas, as had the duke of Medinaceli, but he had to convince Ferdinand and Isabella that his plan was worthy of at least study and, hopefully, a stipend. These concerns must have churned through his mind when inside the great Alcazar of Cordova he walked past the marble columns, the graceful arches that had been built by the Moors and were now in the hands of the Catholic Monarchs. As he approached Queen

Isabella he would have noted that she was very near to his age (she was born in April 1451, he in August or October of the same year), that her hair was the same auburn as his own, her eyes blue like his. Many historians believe that these physical similarities were not unnoticed by Isabella and may have helped create their well-documented affinity for one another. Ferdinand, on the other hand, was slightly younger, and darker in his physical appearance. Columbus bowed before the Catholic Monarchs who were still glowing from their stunning victory over the fall of Malaga. Columbus unfurled a map of the known world and presented his fantastic scheme, stating his mathematical calculations, as he had done in Portugal. He gave an inspired speech about his desire to save souls and to return with enough gems and gold to pay for the rulers' great crusade in Granada as well as for a crusade to liberate the Holy Land. Freeing the Holy Land and Jerusalem was always Columbus's greatest desire, and he repeated many times that it was the single most important reason for his grand scheme. It's almost as if the hope and desire to return to Jerusalem rendered so poignantly by the Jewish poets over the ages was felt just as deeply by Columbus. Indeed, the desire to liberate Jerusalem from the Moors was shared by the Jews and Christians. A devout Catholic, Columbus with Jewish roots most probably would have nursed such a desire. After his grandiose speech the king and queen would not commit themselves to any promises. They did, however, grant him a small stipend while the proposal was referred to a commission.

With the reconquista pressing deeper into Moorish land, the treasury funds were low, leaving precious little for Columbus. Of this first meeting between Columbus and Ferdinand and Isabella, the chronicler, Bernaldez wrote,

"And so Colón came to the Court of King Don Fernando and of Queen Doña Isabel, and he related to them his imagination, to which they did not give much credit [. . .] and he talked to them and told them what he said was true and showed them the world map, so that he put them in desire to know about those lands."[1] Perhaps their generosity in granting him a stipend reflected their own good fortune in war. Malaga had fallen as had Coin, Cartama, Ronda, and Marbella. Ferdinand may have thought that Granada, too, would easily fall into their hands and that within the near future, they would, indeed, be ready to discuss plans for exploration. Ferdinand's policy of retaining his Jewish treasurers, Abravanel and Seneor, in spite of pressure from the Inquisition, was quite literally paying off. Both Abravanel and Seneor had kept the revenues coming in, managing to raise the desperately needed funds for Ferdinand's armies. Madariaga notes, "The King and Queen had to borrow from the private purse of 'some singular persons' amongst their subjects, an euphemism by which cautious Pulgar no doubt quietly suggests that the money came from the two great Jews Don Abraham Seneor and Don Isahak Abarbanel, associate managers of the royal revenue."[2] For the moment, Seneor, Abravanel, and other prominent Jews were quite literally paying for the right of the Jews to remain in Spain.

Columbus's letter of introduction to the king and queen from the duke of Medinaceli had been turned over to Alonso de Quintanilla, Contador Mayor (Chief Royal Treasurer). Quintanilla made three small payments to Columbus even before the royal audience. Excited by the prospect of gold and gems from Columbus's proposed expedition, Quintanilla expedited Columbus's first audience, hoping Ferdinand

and Isabella would immediately grant the expedition. With
the reconquista raging and the constant depletion of funds, it
was decided that a committee should study the proposal just
as it had been studied in Portugal. The commission, headed
by Fray Hernando de Talavera, the queen's confessor,
moved the committee to the University at Salamanca. Madariaga suggests that Talavera, too, was of Jewish descent. He
writes, "Issued from the same Jewish blood . . . Colón and
Talavera incarnated the types of manhood which have stood
for centuries as the models of high achievement respectively
for East and West—the saint and the hero."[3] Roth supports
the claim that Talavera was of Jewish extraction. He writes,
"Juan de Torquemada, Cardinal of San Sisto, was [it was
alleged] of immediate Jewish descent, as were also the
saintly Hernando de Talavera, Archbishop of Granada."[4]
The Torquemada referred to here is not Tomas, the Grand
Inquisitor, but a distant relative. Fray Hernando de Talavera
was the first important person of Jewish extraction Columbus encountered in the Spanish Court, though Talavera did
not lend him his support.

* * *

Who was considered a Converso and how did he differ
from a Marrano and a Jew? A Converso was a man or
woman who converted to Christianity either as a result of a
change in religious belief, a desire for a less restrictive life, or
as a life-saving act. Often during riots Jews had been given
the choice to convert or die and many chose life over death.
In fact, the rabbis reassured the people that God demanded
that one save himself rather than die. A Marrano was a
Converso who ostensibly practiced his Christianity but who
held on to his Jewish beliefs and secretly practiced his Juda-

ism. It was the Marranos, the secret Jews, that the Inquisition was trying to expose. With all the persecution, many
Jews still did not submit to conversion, and paid the exorbitant taxes levied against them for the right to practice their
religion, living with restrictive laws. The relations among the
Jews, Conversos, and Marranos were often strained. The
Jews were very much aware of who the Conversos were and
counted on their support within the Royal Court. Some
Conversos were sensitive and sympathetic to the needs of
their Jewish brethren, but others, particularly some who had
risen within the Church, became hostile, anti-Semitic fanat-
ics. For example, Fray Diego de Deza, from a Converso
family, succeeded Torquemada as Grand Inquisitor and was
almost as relentless in his reign of terror as Torquemada
himself. Jewish families of influence, such as the Abravanels
and Seneors, who enjoyed the wealthy life at Court and who
could represent the Jews, were few and far between. Thus,
jealousy and mistrust were common within these three
groups.

Columbus was not a Converso for, as far as we know,
he, himself, had never converted from Judaism to Christianity. The supposition is that his grandfather had converted.
The question remains, however: was Columbus a Marrano?
Did he at any time actually practice Judaism? Did he ever
attend a Jewish service or practice any of the Jewish rituals?
What knowledge did he have of this possible Jewish ancestry? While most of these questions must go unanswered, we
know that he was surrounded by Conversos, some who
were dogmatic in their Christianity but others who still had
strong Jewish affiliations such as the Sanchez and Santangel
families. We know that Columbus regularly visited one of the
Spanish Juderias, for in his will he left money to the gate-

keeper. Perhaps he went regularly to borrow money, but if he went for a more clandestine purpose, such as attending a Jewish service, then as far as we know, the secret died with him.

Conversos who were high within the court, wielding much power predating Columbus's arrival were Hernando de Pulgar, Secretary to Queen Isabella, and Don Juan Pacheco, Marquis of Villena, who was a confidant to Isabella's brother, King Enrique IV. Besides Fray Hernando de Talavera there were two other prominent Conversos within the church—Salomon ha-Levi, who became Pablo de Santa Maria, Bishop of Burgos, and Fray Diego de Deza.

Fray Diego de Deza was appointed a member of the committee to study Columbus's proposal and, as a result, became one of his most loyal supporters. Kayserling describes de Deza as "a learned theologian of Jewish descent, whom Columbus himself reckons among his most influential patrons and supporters."[5] According to Kayserling, it was de Deza who was responsible for bringing Columbus to the University at Salamanca. Roth also makes note of the Converso de Deza as an influential person in Columbus's life. He states, "Thomas de Torquemada had been succeeded as Grand Inquisitor by the scholarly Diego Deza, the friend and patron of Columbus. Notwithstanding the fact that he himself (like his predecessor) was said to be of Jewish extraction on one side, the activity of the tribunal reached its zenith under his auspices."[6] De Deza seems to have been the first to befriend Columbus when he arrived at Court. Madariaga notes, "Fray Diego de Deza is the first who, from the beginning, wishes him honour and favours him, the first who definitely becomes a partisan on his side."[7] Fray Diego had been a professor of theology at Salamanca, along with Abraham Zacuto. At the university, the commission carefully examined Columbus's mathematics and theories concerning a western route across the sea. The king and queen had ordered that "they should hear Cristóbal Colón with more detail and that they should see the quality of the proposal and the proof he gave that it was possible, that they should confer and discuss upon it, and then should report fully to their Highnesses."[8] Columbus now had to convince the Spanish committee to accept a proposal that had been rejected by the Portuguese. It is important to note that his strongest supporter, even at this early date, was de Deza, from a Converso family.

Columbus was literally encompassed by Conversos, for the king and queen had surrounded themselves with men of Jewish descent. Alonso de Cabrera, a Castilian who had represented Isabella in her marriage arrangements, was a Converso. Roth documents the fact that "Alonso de Cabrera, who belonged to the same class [converso] and was governor of the Alcazar at Segovia, married her [Isabella's] favorite, Beatrize de Bobadilla."[9] Pedro de la Caballeria, another Converso, also helped arrange Ferdinand and Isabella's marriage. According to Kayserling, Caballeria presented Isabella with Ferdinand's gift of the pearl and ruby necklace and even claimed that he paid for the necklace out of his own pocket. Kayserling writes, "Pedro de la Caballeria also had the distinguished honor of presenting to the royal bride, as Ferdinand's nuptial gift, a costly necklace valued at forty thousand ducats, and of paying the whole or large part of its cost."[10] The Caballeria family's Jewish grandfather from the late 1300s was Don Judah de la Caballeria ibn Labi. Two generations later, most of Labi's grandsons had converted, obtaining high offices in Aragon.

According to Kayserling the most important Converso families were: de la Caballeria, Sanchez, and Santangel. The Alfonso de la Caballeria family had, for example, family members who were condemned by the Inquisition, as well as a son who eventually married one of Ferdinand's grand-daughters.[11] From a careful study of these families, it is evident that they walked a fine line between practicing their former Jewish religion and living the powerful life at the Royal Court. Concerning these prominent Converso families, Madariaga writes:

> We know enough about the character of the King and Queen to realise that when the Inquisition showed how widespread was the "heretical depravity" in the ranks of the *Conversos*, they must have been appalled. . . . The names dearest to them, closest to their daily life, were compromised: members of the families associated in their administration glittering in their Courts—La Caballería, Santángel, Sánchez—had to don the penitent's "holy sack" and even to ascend the stake.[12]

Though their very lives were at risk, many of these Conversos had not forsaken their Judaism.

The Sanchez family was second to none in the King's house. Within the family there was Luis, who became president of the highest tribunal in Aragon; Gabriel, who was chief treasurer of Aragon; Guillen, Ferdinand's cup bearer; and Francisco, who was a steward in Ferdinand's household.[13] It seems that most of Ferdinand's men were Conversos. Roth points out, "The proudest nobility contracted family alliances with the wealthy conversos. So did the Henriquez family, to which the mother of Ferdinand the Catholic belonged."[14] Columbus was surrounded by powerful Conversos who understood what it was like to be of Jewish descent in the Catholic Court. When Columbus reverted to his former family name of Colon, he may have been signaling these Conversos that he, too, was of Jewish extraction. The subliminal message was probably not lost, for these Conversos became his strongest advocates in the Royal Court.

The single most influential Converso who helped Columbus's enterprise get under way was Luis de Santangel, Escribano de Racion, Ferdinand's Budget Minister. Santangel's older cousin, for whom he had been named, was beheaded and then burned for his supposed part in the murder of Fray Pedro Arbues, an inquisitor in Saragossa.[15] This murder, along with the subsequent autos de fé, set in motion a series of events that eventually led to the final expulsion of the Jews and, to some degree, Columbus's expedition.

In April of 1484 the Inquisition's tribunal was established in Aragon. On June 3, 1485, two Conversos were burned at the stake in Saragossa. Autos de fé had already been raging throughout Castile, but prominent Conversos in Aragon were determined to stop the dreaded Inquisition from spreading into their land. A plot was devised at the home of Luis de Santangel (the high treasurer's older cousin) to assassinate the Inquisitor, Fray Pedro Arbues, who had condemned the victims of the auto de fé. On September 15, 1485, Arbues was assassinated in the Cathedral in Saragossa. Two hundred Conversos were named as conspirators. Luis de Santangel, the King's treasurer, was also named, but he escaped. Juan Pedro Sanchez and Alfonso de la Caballeria, Ferdinand's most trusted men, were also implicated. Santangel's cousin was caught, beheaded, and then burned in an auto de fé. Alfonso de la Caballeria obtained protection from Rome but his wife was a penitent in an auto de fé.[16] Walter F. McEntire claims:

> The conspirators—all Marranos—were Sancho de Paternoy, chief treasurer of Aragon, "who had his own seat in the synagogue of Saragossa"; Alfonso de la Caballeria, vice-chancellor of Aragon; Juan Pedro Sanchez, Pedro de Almazan, Pedro Monfort, Juan de la Abadia, Mateo Ram, Notary Garcia de Moros, Pedro de Vera, and others resident in Saragossa, Calatayud and Barbastro.[17]

It is interesting that McEntire notes that these men were Marranos, not just Conversos. His insinuation is that the men in the conspiracy were not just trying to stop the Inquisition from taking hold in Aragon but were all actively practicing Judaism.

The Inquisition tortured everyone connected with the Arbues assassination. Roth records that "a large number of the conversos of the city were virtually in its hands, to condemn when it pleased. The names of the great families of Santángel and Sánchez appear with monotonous regularity in its records."[18] During this fiery time of swelling hatred and mistrust, of tribunals and autos de fé, Columbus waited for the commission in Salamanca to come to a decision concerning his proposal. It must have been a doubly anxious time for him, because even as the families of Santangel, Caballeria, and Sanchez were being investigated, so too were the Coloms of Spain.

7

COLUMBUS AND THE MARRANOS— SECRET JEWS

1484–1489

A heretic dressed in the Sanbenito, condemned to be burned at an auto de fé.

On festival days, processions were led by the clergy, who paraded into the city square where seats were arranged around the perimeter, and a temporary altar was erected. Behind the clergy marched the penitents who were dressed in Sanbenitos (yellow sacks painted with devils and flames), wearing pointed caps of shame and walking barefoot. The condemned Marranos followed. Some were carried in cages, for their injuries from the torture chambers left them deformed and immobile. Those who could walk held lit green candles. The sentences were read, and the condemned were marched out beyond the city gates to the quemadero, the place where the stakes were prepared for the auto de fé. The actual death by fire was carried out by the secular law, for after judgment was passed by the

Church, the condemned were "relaxed" or turned over to the secular law enforcers. The justification for this method of death by fire came from the New Testament (John 15:6): "If a man abide not in me, he is cast forth as a branch and is withered: and men gather them and cast them into the fire, and they are burned."[1] Armed with this biblical passage, the collective population turned the act of faith into a macabre spectacle. Hundreds of people came to watch and window seats around the square could be bought for a high price. Hordes of people threw rotten tomatoes and eggs at the victims, spat on them, and shouted obscenities as they passed. Priests beseeched them to recant, crying, "Receive the sign of the cross which ye have denied and lost."[2] If the condemned Marranos recanted and embraced Christianity, they were granted death by strangulation before being consigned to the flames. Few recanted. Most of the men and women bravely walked to the stakes and were tied there. It was considered an honor for an esteemed member of the nobility to light one of the pyres. But, often, as the flames roared up, the Marranos would lift their faces to the darkening sky and recite, "*Shema Yisrael Adonai Eloheinu, Adonai Ehad!*" then die as martyrs.

Though Marranos were well entrenched in the Royal Court, they were just as helpless as the Jews in fighting the Inquisition but, indeed, they did fight. The Pedro Arbues murder was one example of their striking back. It was the Conversos, from the earliest days of Isabella's reign, who backed the Queen and helped her ascend the throne, often clashing with King Enrique's men. During the late reign of Enrique, the Spains were divided between Old Christians and New Christians, between Enrique's men and Isabella's. Though Isabella would not seize the crown because of her firm belief in the divine right to rule, Abraham Seneor, with the aid of other Conversos, managed to secure Segovia for her in 1473. As Baer notes, "There was good reason for the mutual understanding that existed between the young rulers and their helpers of Jewish descent. Both Jews and conversos with Jewish sympathies were inclined to support a strong regime that would maintain law and order in the country and to overlook at first the possible consequences from their religious viewpoint."[3] When Enrique died, Isabella finally accepted the crown. In an effort to bring law and order to the chaotic state that Enrique had left as his legacy, Isabella and Ferdinand consolidated their power, heard judicial cases themselves, and established a strong police force, the Hermandad. From the earliest days of their rule, the Catholic Monarchs made distinctions between the Jews and the Conversos. For the time being they were content to leave the Jews alone, making good use of their talents as tax farmers, craftsmen, and physicians. Heresy, however, particularly the heresy of a relapsed Converso to Judaism, was something they would not tolerate. Under the Catholic Monarchs' auspices the Inquisition began to grow more powerful. But, as Baer states, "the Christian reforms were not, in fact, intended to undermine the ancient rights of the Jewish community. . . ."[4] The Inquisition was not established, at first, as an anti-Semitic organization bent on the destruction of the Jews of Spain. In fact, however, that is what it ultimately became.

In the Catholic Monarchs' early reign, the Jews and Conversos were much appreciated. Abraham Seneor was rewarded for his loyalty in their marriage arrangements and in securing Segovia. He was made treasurer-general of the Hermandad. Seneor's son-in-law, Meir Melamed, was one of the chief administrators of tax farming, or tax collecting. Don Isaac Abravanel and his son-in-law, Joseph Abravanel, were also quickly corralled into the Royal Court shortly after their arrival in 1483. The Conversos Cavalleria, Sanchez, Santangel and Cabrera were well entrenched within the Court in the 1470s and early 1480s, but the heat of the autos de fé would be felt soon throughout all the Spains.

On November 1, 1478, Pope Sixtus IV issued a bull that enabled Ferdinand and Isabella to expand the work of the tribunals, and the insidious work of torturing victims for information began in earnest. From its inception there were three types of torture that were commonly used to force a confession of Judaizing from a victim. First, the victims were stripped naked. The rope torture consisted of tying the victim's hands behind him, his arms extended backwards. He was raised to the ceiling and then dropped in sudden jerks, causing excruciating pain as limbs were dislocated. The water torture procedure placed the victim into a moveable trough and forced him to swallow jugs of water, sometimes as many as six. Then the sides of the trough were pressed in. A bar underneath the victim would break his back. If no confession was forthcoming, a wet rag was placed over the nose and mouth and water was poured over them. Victims would suck in the soaked rag, choking, and suddenly the rag would be yanked out, often tearing the soft tissue of the throat and mouth. The third torture was the use of fire applied to the feet. Over the three hundred years of the Inquisition, other methods of torture were devised. Some victims were tied to stretching wheels, and others were hung like sides of beef. These were but a few of the tortures used. The very worst of human nature was unleashed in the creation and use of these tortures. Often, even the most stalwart would collapse and names of beloved family members and friends would escape their lips.[5]

The terrible irony behind all of this was that prior to 1492, the Marranos could be sentenced to the stake for not eating pork, for not cooking on the Jewish Sabbath, for preparing a single meal with Jewish rituals, and for eating matzah, while their Jewish counterparts were allowed to practice their religion. The Inquisition was determined to root out heretics who professed to be Christians but were really Marranos. The *Edict of Faith* listed all the offenses for which a person could be arrested.

If they observe the Sabbath, putting on clean or festive clothes, clean and washed shirts and headdress; arranging and cleaning their houses on Friday afternoon, and in the evening lighting new candles, with new tapers and torches, earlier than on other evenings of the week; cooking on the said Fridays such food as is required for the Saturday, and on the latter eating the meat thus cooked on the Friday, as is the manner of the Jews; keeping the Jewish fasts, not touching food the whole day until nightfall, and especially the Fast of Queen Ester, and the chief fast of *Cinquepur* [Fast of Atonement] and other Jewish fasts, laid down by their Law; and keeping other fasts in the week, especially Mondays and Thursdays, kept by them as devotional fasts; eating on [the conclusion of?] such fast days such meats and other viands as are customary with the Jews; and on the said fast days asking pardon of one another in the Jewish manner, the younger ones to the elders, the latter placing their hands on the heads of the former, but without signing them with the sign of the Cross; . . . keeping the feasts and festivals of the Jews, in particular the feast of unleavened bread, which falls in Holy Week,

upon which festival they eat unleavened bread, beginning their meal with lettuce and celery; keeping the feast
of Tabernacles which falls in the month of September;
saying Jewish prayers . . . reciting these with the face
turned to the wall, moving the head backwards and
forwards as the Jews do; cutting the nails and keeping,
burning or burying the parings; cleansing, or causing
meat to be cleaned, cutting away from it all fat and
grease, and cutting away the nerve or sinew from the
leg; cutting the throats of fowls as is the manner of the
Jews, reciting certain words during the process and
passing the knife across the nail; killing oxen as the
Jews do, covering the blood with cinders or with earth;
giving the Jewish blessing before eating, called the
baraha; reciting certain words over the cup or vase of
wine, after which each person sips a little, according to
the custom of the Jews; not eating pork, hare, rabbit,
strangled birds, conger-eel, cuttlefish, nor eels or other
scaleless fish, as laid down in Jewish law; and upon the
death of parents and others eating, on the floor or on
very low tables, such things as boiled eggs, olives, and
other viands, as do the Jews; . . . pouring water from
jars and pitchers when someone had died, believing that
the soul of such persons will come and bathe in the
water; and who when kneading bread will throw parti-
cles of dough in the fire, which the Jews call *Hallah*;
making divinations for children born to them, on the
seventh day; not baptizing them, and when they have
been baptized scraping off the chrism put on them in
the sacrament of baptism; . . . If they give Old Testament names to the children, or bless them by the laying
on of hands; if the women do not attend Church within
forty days after a confinement; if the dying turn towards
the wall; if they wash a corpse with warm water; if they
recite the Psalms without adding the *Gloria Patri* at the
close; who say that the dead Law of Moses is good, and

can bring about their salvation, and perform other rites
and ceremonies of the same.[6]

Not all the names that came before the tribunal were
dragged out of the tortured. Jealous neighbors, people who
bore grudges against Conversos, or even servants within
their homes could bring names of Marranos to the Inquisitors, who were quick to arrest the suspects.

In August of 1481, the plague broke out in Seville and
many Conversos fled, fearing that they would be blamed for
the epidemic, as indeed they were. During the plague, a
number of prominent Conversos, who did not flee, feared
that many of them would be brought before the tribunal.
They arranged a resistance to the tribunal, its torture
chambers, and threats of autos de fé. One man was quoted
as saying, "How can they come against us? We are the
principal members of the city, and well liked by the people.
Let us assemble our men. If they come to take us, we will set
the city in a turmoil, with our followers and our friends."[7]
One of the leaders of this group was Diego de Susan, a
wealthy merchant. His daughter, who was nicknamed La
Susanna, knew all the details of the revolt and, in a weak
moment of misplaced trust, whispered the plans to her
young Christian lover. The young man immediately reported
the information to the tribunal. All of the leaders, including
Diego de Susan, were arrested. On February 6, 1481, six
men and women died as martyrs in an auto de fé, and Diego
Susan died in a second one. La Susanna was sent to a
convent but was so distracted with grief that she fled, and for
the rest of her sad, short life, lived in disgrace. On her
deathbed, she asked that her skull be placed over the door-

way of her father's house so that all should know her shame and remember what had happened. Her request was honored, and because of the horror which had occurred there the street was called the Street of Death.[8]

On October 17, 1483, Pope Sixtus IV appointed Tomas de Torquemada Grand Inquisitor, head of the Counsel of the Supreme and General Inquisition. His fanatical reign whipped up a tempest of terror. Between the years 1481 and 1488, 750 men and women in Seville alone were burned in autos de fé. In Toledo 900 penitents at a time walked bareheaded and barefoot to the Cathedral. Mobs jeered and humiliated them. Some of the condemned wept, while others bravely faced their deaths. In 1486 over 5,000 penitents marched in the Toledo processions. It was recorded that over fifty people at a time were burned at different autos de fé. Andres Bernaldez recorded that

> All of them . . . were Jews, and clung to their hope, like the Israelites in Egypt, who suffered many blows at the hands of the Egyptians and yet believed that God would lead them out of the midst of them, as He did with a mighty hand and an outstretched arm. So, too, the *conversos* looked upon the Christians as Egyptians or worse, and believed that God had them in His keeping and preserved them as by a miracle. . . . The Inquisition proposed to destroy both their belief and the believers. "The fire has been kindled, and it will burn until not one of them is left alive."[9]

The fires burned in all the Spains. In Seville, Cordova, Toledo, Burgos, Segovia, Ciudad Real, Saragossa, Teruel, and Tarragona the autos de fé took place. It is calculated that the Judaizers put to death by the Inquisition in Spain and Portugal during its three hundred years of activity probably totaled more than 30,000.[10] What at first seemed to be an acceptable way of living within the Catholic society (and one must not forget that many of these conversions were performed under duress) quickly led to great jeopardy for the Marranos. They were hunted by the Church and scorned by the Jews who had none of the benefits of being Conversos. For the most part, the Jews considered the Conversos to be traitors.

At first King Ferdinand and Queen Isabella adamantly argued that the Jews were not being molested by the Inquisition and, to some extent, this was true. However, any Jew whose name was mentioned in the torture chamber as having seduced a Converso back to his old religion was immediately arrested and then faced the slow, agonizing death of stoning or being roasted on a spit. In truth, the establishment of the Inquisition represented the prelude to the final explusion of the Jews from Spain.

Kol Nidrei, the heartrending, mournful prayer of the Day of Atonement, is said to have grown out of the despair of the Marranos, the Spanish martyrs and the Jews sent into exile. The *Encyclopaedia Judaica* states,

Kol Nidrei's persistent popularity is partly attributed to the emotional factors, especially its association with the Jewish Martyrdom. In 1917, Joseph S. Block propounded a dramatic, though unsubstantiated, theory that Kol Nidrei arose as a reaction to forced Jewish conversions to Christianity by the Visigoths in seventh-

century Spain, to persecutions in the Byzantine Empire
(700–850), and in Spain to persecutions by the Inquisition (1391–1492).[11]

It is significant to note that the prayers are a disavowal of
oaths made under duress, such as the vows the Conversos
were forced to make in fifteenth-century Spain. Even if the
haunting Kol Nidrei did not evolve from the misery of this
period, it poignantly reflects the despair the Marranos and
Jews felt during this time of unrelenting persecution.

* * *

In 1489, in Tarragona, a city on the Mediterranean coast
of Catalonia, Andres Colom, Blanca Colom and Francisca
Colom were accused of relapsing to Judaism. They had
observed Jewish rites. Some twenty years before this,
Thome Colom, Leonore Colom, their son Joam, and his wife
Aldonza had buried Thome's mother-in-law in the Jewish
fashion in Valencia. They had all died in an auto de fé. Now,
in 1489, as Columbus waited in Salamanca for a decision on
his proposal, this second Colom family was on trial before
the Tarragona tribunal.[12]

Upon his arrival in Portugal, Columbus used the name
Colom. Madariaga states that, "in Portugal, he seems to
have gone straight over to the Colom and Colón, for Barroa,
King John's historian, calls him Colom . . . yet, in Castille
. . . his name is always Colomo. . . . It evinces a kind of
caution lest Colom might prove dangerous in King Ferdinand's realms. . . . The first time Colón is allowed to see the
light is when . . . the discoverer drafts his Capitulations."[13]
One must ask several questions. First, why didn't Columbus

use the name Colombo if he had pride in his Genoese background? Second, why was he constantly changing his name? By stylizing himself Don Cristobal Colon, he might have felt Colon was a safer name than Colom. Knowing that Coloms were on trial in Tarragona, it becomes clearer why he would not go by that name. The acceptance for his proposal was tenuous at best, and an Inquisitional investigation would certainly have destroyed any chance he might have had. One can only imagine Columbus's thoughts when news reached him that the Coloms had been found guilty of heresy and had died in an auto de fé in Tarragona, Catalonia, the land from which his own grandparents may have fled.

8

A MATTER OF FUNDS

1492

The Edict of Expulsion signed by Ferdinand and Isabella. Photocopy by Ernest Maass. Reprinted by permission of Ann Maass. Photo courtesy of Robert Sugar.

S lumped forward in his saddle, his graying red head hanging low, Columbus rode out of Santa Fe after he was formally rejected by the Royal Committee in early January 1492. He had presented his plan, his calculations, and his maps but to no avail. The royal coffers were empty. Once again there simply was not enough money for a risky enterprise. His heart was so heavy with disappointment that he had finally made up his mind to join his brother, Bartholomew, at Charles VIII's Court in France. Perhaps there he would finally find a Royal Court to sponsor him. Accompanied by Fray Juan Perez, he was crossing the bridge at Pinos-Puente when he was overtaken by royal guards recalling him to Santa Fe. Incredulous, he turned his mule around and began a journey that would ultimately lead him to the New World.

* * *

The six years of waiting for royal approval had been fraught with financial trouble and humiliation. He had often been the brunt of crude jokes, noblemen asking him if he was planning on sailing to the moon. He knew they thought he was mad.

He lived in Cordova during this period and took comfort in his relationship with Beatriz Enriquez de Harana. He probably met her sometime in 1487, and though they never married, they had a son, Fernando, who was born on August 15, 1488. It is possible that Beatriz came from a Converso family. Her father's real name was Torquemada. Madariaga writes, "that was the name of a famous Converso family, that of Don Juan de Torquemada, Cardinal of St. Sixt, to which it would appear the famous Inquisitor-General belonged also."[1] Though the Enriquez family may have been distantly related to Tomas Torquemada, their use of the name Enriquez suggests their intense dislike and perhaps fear and hatred for the infamous Grand Inquisitor.

Desperate for funds and anxious to set out to sea, in 1487, Columbus had written to King Joao, who answered, "And as you might perhaps harbour a certain distrust towards our justices owing to obligations which you may have, We by this letter, guarantee you that during your coming stay and return, you shall not be arrested, held up, accused, remanded or made to answer for any thing, whether civil or criminal, of any kind."[2] Madariaga suggests that King Joao was referring to Columbus's knowledge and perhaps possession of the secret Toscanelli letter, assuring Joao that the East could be reached by sailing west. With the failure of the earlier attempt by Captains Dulmo and Estreito, King Joao obviously wished to confer with Columbus once again. Also, Joao may have been anxious to entice Columbus away from the Spanish Court, lest Ferdinand grant him the expedition. Columbus returned to Portugal, arriving in Lisbon just as Bartholomew Diaz received a hero's welcome from his glorious trip to the Cape of Good Hope in December 1487. With all the excitement centered around Diaz, King Joao once again lost interest in Columbus.

Around this time, King Henry VII of England expressed a desire to meet Columbus, so his brother, Bartholomew, traveled north while Christopher returned to Spain. When King Henry seemed unable to make a commitment, Bartholomew traveled on to France. Here at Fontainebleau, Bartholomew made a strong impression on Charles VIII's sister, Anne de Beaujeu. To his chagrin, however, he was put to work as a cartographer, and a decision on the enterprise was delayed indefinitely.

King Ferdinand must have known that Columbus's brother was at Charles's court and worried that he might lose Columbus to the French. Why then didn't Ferdinand give Columbus permission to sail in 1487? Though all the royal funds were diverted for the war in Granada, there were wealthy men who could have lent money to the Crown for the enterprise. After all, if Columbus's voyage was successful, Spain would have the only ocean route to the East, with access to the tremendous wealth such a route would make available. One must question whether Ferdinand and Isabella suspected that Columbus may have been of Jewish extraction and that perhaps this was the reason they procrastinated and then outright rejected him. Madariaga suggests that Columbus's Converso background was, indeed, an embarrassment to the Catholic Monarchs. While they didn't want him to leave for France, they were ambivalent about financing him themselves. Madariaga states, "Ferdinand must have secured all the information he wished about this family [Columbus], and must therefore have known that they were of Catalan-Jewish origin."[3] Madariaga goes on to suggest that the Catholic Monarchs were so aware of Columbus's background that they never once referred to his nationality but always to him as "the foreigner." By 1491, it seems, the Royal Court in general ridiculed him. The Royal Commission's opinions were that "his promises and offers had been judged by the King and Queen to be impossible and vain and worthy of all rejection."[4] The commission was so negative they concluded that Ferdinand and Isabella would be making a foolish mistake should they sponsor the enterprise. The Commission wrote:

> It was not in the interest of the authority of their royal persons that they should give their support to a business so weakly founded and which was bound to seem uncertain and impossible to any well-educated person, however lacking in expert knowledge, for they would lose their money invested in it as well as their royal authority without reaping any advantage.[5]

Columbus must have been very despondent at this point, for he left Santa Fe and returned to La Rabida where Fray Juan Perez continued to encourage him. It seems that now, for the first time, Columbus finally revealed his knowledge of the secret Toscanelli letter to Perez. Perez immediately wrote to the king and queen. Whether they presented this new evidence to the Commission is unclear. However, from this point on, no one ever again questioned the feasibility of sailing west to reach the East. The information in Toscanelli's letter must finally have put an end to all the skepticism. Columbus was once again recalled to Santa Fe.

* * *

Two stumbling blocks to the enterprise remained. When Columbus returned to Court his demands concerning an admiralty and 10 percent of profits were considered insolent. There was still the serious question of lack of funds. Since the Crown had no money, it would have to come from somewhere else.

It is difficult to imagine how Columbus could have had the audacity to stride into the throne room after being so despondent and then proceed to make such extravagant demands. It seems he felt he deserved to be styled a Don and Admiral of the Ocean Sea because of the other admiral (the suggested Admiral Casenove-Coullon) in his family. This point caused King Ferdinand to bristle. Columbus also demanded to be appointed viceroy and Governor-General over any lands he would discover. He proposed to keep one-tenth of all material goods such as gold, silver, gems, pearls, and spices and demanded one-eighth of all goods on other expeditions.[6] Ferdinand was outraged and rejected him utterly. Columbus packed his saddlebags and headed for Cordova. From there he planned to travel on to France. What transpired between his abrupt dismissal and his subsequent recall changed the entire course of history.

* * *

At this momentous time, Columbus's life was inextricably intertwined with the Jews of Spain. A closer look at the political and religious intrigues provides some explanations of critical decisions made by Ferdinand and Isabella in the month of January 1492. A year and a half before, in the summer of 1490, four men were arrested in separate incidents for Judaizing. They were Benito Garcia, Yuce and Juan Franco, and Juan de Ocana. Under torture, they confessed to having practiced black magic in an effort to stop the Inquisition. The magic included the crucifixion of a child from La Guardia, a town in the province of Toledo. Baer meticulously examined the tribunal records concerning the La Guardia case and notes that "the charges of sorcery and child-crucifixion were the inventions of antisemitic propaganda . . . practically every word touching on the matter of the crimes is demonstrably false."[7] None of the testimonies matched. The time, date, and place of the crime were all different. No child was ever found to be missing from La Guardia, and the Inquisition never made any attempt to uncover the identity of the missing child. They never looked for the child's supposed grave. No member of the Jewish community was allowed to explain that the Jews did not practice magic nor were any Jews allowed come to the defendants' aid. Baer suggests that Torquemada, who was the judge in this case, released the trial proceedings just as he was building the momentum to have the Jews expelled from Spain. Baer writes, "when the records of the trial were first published, some modern scholars suggested that the inquisitor general had staged it so as to prepare the public for the wholesale expulsion of the Jews from Spain, which was decreed three months after the trial's end. . . .only the very naive . . . can ignore the historical links between the La Guardia trial and the Expulsion."[8] The impact of the La Guardia trial upon Queen

Isabella was enormous. She was horrified by the confessions of the victims and began to feel that the Jews were becoming a dangerous element within the state. It may seem incredible, 500 years later, that black magic was considered a serious threat to the state, but it must be remembered that the Inquisition had the full support of Ferdinand and Isabella. Torquemada was held in their highest esteem. The Catholic Monarchs did not question the tribunal's findings.

On November 4, 1491, the four condemned men were relaxed to the secular law and burned in an auto de fé. This occurred a little over one month before the fall of Granada. Torquemada's timing for a spectacular case and spectacular auto de fé could not have been better planned. With the Moors finally conquered, there was now an emotional issue upon which to base the expulsion of the Jews. Cecil Roth also acknowledges the tremendous impact the La Guardia trial had on the decision to expel the Jews. Roth notes, "The episode, wholly fictitious though its basis was, provided a fresh weapon against the Jews, which Torquemada did not scruple to use. . . . Moreover, the growing degradation and impoverishment of the Jews had rendered nugatory the material advantages which their presence had formerly conferred upon the State. They could be dispensed without misgiving and without loss."[9] Besides the emotional, religious fervor to expel the Jews, there was an even more pressing factor. The Crown needed funds.

One solution to financing the Columbus enterprise would be to borrow money, but then the creditors (the duke of Medinaceli in particular) would have a large share in any of the profits. The other solution, expulsion of the Jews and confiscation of their properties, would give Ferdinand access to the millions of maravedis he needed. As Kayserling notes,

> Ferdinand was led to adopt this measure more by the economic and political reasons, more by the desire to promote his own material interests, than by the religious zeal which actuated Isabella. The king needed plenty of money to carry out his plan of bringing new territory under his dominion. He took it from the Jews, who were wealthy, especially in Castile; some of them were worth as much as one or two million maravedis or more.[10]

The expulsion of the Jews was certainly a drastic step to take. Now Ferdinand consulted with his most trusted men from Aragon, all of whom were Conversos.

Within the time Columbus had been dismissed and was preparing to leave for Cordova, then France, the Conversos Gabriel Sanchez, Alonso de la Caballeria, and Alonso de Cabrera closeted themselves with King Ferdinand and discussed the importance of the enterprise. One would have to guess that the pressing issue was the advantage King Charles would have should he sponsor Columbus. As kingsmen from Aragon, they, like the king himself, would not want an enriched Charles, a Charles who would then have the means to retake Roussillon and other provinces. But the most influential Converso, who also met privately with the king and queen, was Luis de Santangel. It was Santangel who finally convinced Ferdinand to reconsider Columbus's proposal. When he offered to finance the entire enterprise with his own funds, Isabella refused him and proposed to pawn her jewels. Santangel assured her that it would not be necessary, that a number of other options existed. He argued that even if the Crown borrowed the money for the enterprise, the Crown would still be the main beneficiary of any discoveries. Don Isaac Abravanel was one of the names mentioned as a source for money. As Kayserling notes, "Isaac Abravanel was one of the first to render financial assistance to Columbus's undertaking."[11] One can guess that Santangel (a Converso who was forced to march as a penitent in an auto de fé and who had strong Jewish sympathies) may have been trying to plea bargain for the Jews, assuring the Crown that monies could be raised without the drastic step of expulsion. Abravanel must also have recognized the pressing need to keep Columbus in Spain and perhaps, even at this early date in January, must have had some sense that once the monies for Columbus's voyage were raised there would be less pressure to expel the Jews. Kayserling notes:

> Santangel is credited with an item of 1,140,000 maravedis which he gave to the bishop of Avila for Columbus's expedition. . . . Luis de Santangel, the king's *escribano de racion*, whose authorization was presented with the aforesaid order, 2,640,000 maravedis, to wit, 1,500,000 in payment to Isaac Abravanel of money which he had lent their majesties in the Moorish War, and the remaining 1,140,000 maravedis in payment to the aforesaid *escribano de racion* of money which he advanced to equip the caravels ordered by their majesties for the expedition to the Indies and to pay Christopher Columbus, the admiral of that fleet.[12]

Together Santangel and Abravanel seemed to be trying to avert an edict of expulsion in tandem with the financial planning for Columbus's expedition. Ferdinand's Converso counselors finally persuaded him to give in to Columbus's demands and the formation of plans to finance the expedition were under way. Columbus was recalled to Court.

However, the plot to expel the Jews from Spain was still under consideration. The Jews must have known that the possibility existed but still they did not believe the Catholic Monarchs would really issue such an edict. The royal contracts for the Jewish treasurers Abraham Seneor, Meir Melamed, Don Isaac Abravanel and Joseph Abravanel had been renewed. This in itself was reassuring. It was a false security, however, for even as the contracts were being renewed, the king and queen were hoping to convince these prominent men to convert. It was quite evident that expulsion plans were well underway along with the Monarchs' intention to keep Seneor, Abravanel, and their families in Spain. Baer writes:

> The last acts of the Catholic Monarchs in this respect give a clue to their original intention to convert these excellent men and so retain them in the service of the State even after the Expulsion. In December 1491, the sovereigns enacted new laws for the reform of the system of tax-farming, reserving to themselves full rights of supervision and also the right to cancel contracts inconsistent with the reorganization plans of the State.[13]

It is clear that the Catholic Monarchs had every intention of accomplishing complete unity between Church and State from the time Granada was conquered. Isabella's strong faith in her Divine Right to rule led her to believe that God had given them this great religious victory, and that the new State had to be dedicated to Him. Certainly Ferdinand knew that with the expulsion of the Jews the Crown would not have to borrow money for the enterprise, or share any of the profits. On March 30, 1492, the Catholic Monarchs issued the Edict of Expulsion. On April 30, 1492, the same day the Edict was formally announced across the land, Columbus was ordered to ready himself for his expedition. Kayserling makes the connection between these two great historic events.

> On April 30, the very day on which the expulsion of the Jews was everywhere publicly announced, Columbus was ordered to equip a fleet for his voyage to the Indies, and at the same time he received the contract which on April 17th had been arranged in Santa Fe between him and Juan de Columa, the latter acting on behalf of the Spanish sovereigns. Ferdinand, who had long energetically opposed the expedition, was obliged to yield, thanks to Columbus's persistency, and was obliged to accept the explorer's excessive demands, which had twice caused the negotiations to be discontinued.[14]

Madariaga also notes the fact that these two historic events were announced on the same day.

> On that very day, the man who had signed the decree expelling the Jews had put his signature to two all-important papers in the history of the discovery of America—by the first, Colon was granted the titles and dignities which had been stipulated in the Capitulations; by the second, the King and Queen reminded Diego

Rodriguez Prieto, Alcalde Mayor of Palos, and "All other persons your companions and neighbors of the Borough of Palos," that they had been sentenced by the Council to serve the King and Queen with two caravels armed at their expense for two years, and commanded them to put the said caravels at the disposal of Cristóbal Colón to go to "certain parts of the Ocean Sea on some errands required by our service."[15]

The race to raise instant money for Columbus's enterprise was on. Abravanel and Seneor began a desperate collection of funds to bring before the king, for now, what finally hung in the balance was the right of the Jews to remain in Spain.

9

THE EXPULSION

March 30–August 2, 1492

Sketch of the Santa Maria by Joaquín Sorolla y Bastida (1863–1923). Courtesy of the Hispanic Society of America.

*Edict of Ferdinand and Isabella for the Expulsion of the Jews,
dated Granada, 30th March, 1492*

Whereas, having been informed that in these our kingdoms, there were some bad Christians who judaized and apos-
tatized from our holy catholic faith, the chief cause of which
was the communication of Jews with Christians; at the Cortes
we held in the city of Toledo in the year 1480, we ordered the
said Jews in all the cities, towns, and places in our kingdoms
and dominions, to separate into Jewries and places apart,
where they should live and reside, hoping by their separation
alone to remedy the evil. Furthermore, we have sought and
given orders, that inquisition should be made in our said kingdoms, which, as is known, for upwards of twelve years has
been, and is done, whereby many guilty persons have been
discovered, as is notorious. And as we are informed by the
inquisitors, and many other religious, ecclesiastical, and secular
persons, that great injury has resulted, and does result, and it is
stated, and appears to be, from the participation, society, and
communication they held and do hold with Jews, who it appears always endeavour in every way they can to subvert our
holy catholic faith, and to make faithful Christians withdraw
and separate themselves therefrom, and attract and pervert
them to their injurious opinions and belief, instructing them in
the ceremonies and observances of their religion, holding meet-
ings where they read and teach them what they are to believe
and observe according to their religion; seeking to circumcise
them and their children; giving them books from which they
may read their prayers; and explaining to them the fasts they
are to observe; assembling with them to read and to teach them
the histories of their law; notifying to them the festivals previous

to their occurring, and instructing them what they are to do and observe thereon; giving and carrying to them from their houses unleavened bread, and meat slaughtered with ceremonies; instructing them what they are to refrain from, as well in food as in other matters, for the due observance of their religion, and persuading them all they can to profess and keep the law of Moses; giving them to understand, that except that, there is no other law or truth, which is proved by many declarations and confessions, as well of Jews themselves as of those who have been perverted and deceived by them, which has greatly redounded to the injury, detriment, and opprobrium of our holy catholic faith.

Notwithstanding we were informed of the major part of this before, and we knew the certain remedy for all these injuries and inconveniences was to separate the said Jews from all communications with Christians, and banish them from all our kingdoms, yet we were desirous to content ourselves by ordering them to quit all the cities, towns, and places of Andalusia, where, it appears, they had done the greatest mischief, considering that would suffice, and that those of other cities, towns and places would cease to do and commit the same.

But as we are informed that neither that, nor the execution of some of the said Jews, who have been guilty of the said crimes and offences against our holy Catholic faith, has been sufficient for a complete remedy to obviate and arrest so great an opprobrium and offence to the Catholic faith and religion.

And as it is found and appears, that the said Jews, wherever they live and congregate, daily increase in continuing their wicked and injurious purposes; to afford them no further opportunity for insulting our holy Catholic faith, and those whom until now God has been pleased to preserve, as well as those who had fallen, but have amended and are brought back to our holy mother church, which, according to the weakness of our human nature and the diabolical suggestion that continually wages war with us, may easily occur, unless the principal cause of it be removed, which is to banish the said Jews from our kingdoms.

And when any serious and detestable crime is committed by some persons of a college or university, it is right that such college or university should be dissolved and annihilated, and the lesser suffer for the greater, and one be punished for the other; and those that disturb the welfare and proper living of cities and towns, that by contagion may injure others, should be expelled therefrom, and even for lighter causes that might be injurious to the state, how much more then for the greatest, most dangerous, and contagious of crimes like this.

Therefore, we, by and with the counsel and advice of some prelates and high noblemen of our kingdoms, and other learned persons of our council, having maturely deliberated thereon, resolve to order all the said Jews and Jewesses to quit our kingdoms, and never to return or come back to them, or any of them. Therefore we command this our edict to be issued, whereby we command all Jews and Jewesses, of whatever age they may be, that live, reside, and dwell in our said kingdoms and dominions, as well natives as those who are not, who in any manner or for any cause may have come to dwell therein, that by the end of the month of July next, of the present year 1492, they depart from all our said kingdoms and dominions, with their sons, daughters, man-servants, maidservants, and Jewish attendants, both great and small, of whatever age they may be; and they shall not presume to return to, nor reside therein, or in any part of them, either as residents, travellers, or in any other manner whatever, under pain that if they do not perform and execute the same, and are found to reside in our said kingdoms and dominions, or should in any manner live therein, they incur the penalty of death, and confiscation of all their property to our treasury, which penalty they incur by the act itself, without further process, declaration, or sentence.

And we command and forbid any person or persons of our said kingdoms, of whatsoever rank, station, or condition they may be, that they do not presume publicly or secretly to receive, shelter, protect, or defend any Jew or Jewess, after the said term of the end of July, in their lands or houses, or in any other part of our said kingdoms and dominions, henceforward for ever and ever, under pain of losing all their property, vassals, castles, and other possessions; and furthermore forfeit to our treasury any sums they have, or receive from us.

And that the said Jews and Jewesses during the said time, until the end of the said month of July, may be the better able to dispose of themselves, their property, and estates, we hereby take and receive them under our security, protection, and royal safeguard; and insure to them and their properties, that during the said period, until the said day, the end of the said month of July, they may travel in safety, and may enter, sell, barter, and alienate all their moveable and immoveable property, and freely dispose thereof at their pleasure.

And that during the said time, no harm, injury, or wrong whatever shall be done to their persons or properties contrary to justice, under the pains those persons incur and are liable to, that violate our royal safeguard.

We likewise grant permission and authority to the said Jews and Jewesses, to export their wealth and property, by sea or land, from our said kingdoms and dominions, provided they do not take away gold, silver, money, or other articles prohibited by the laws of our kingdoms, but in merchandise and goods that are not prohibited.

And we command all the justices of our kingdoms, that they cause the whole of the above herein contained to be observed and fulfilled, and that they do not act contrary hereto; and that they afford all necessary favour, under pain of being deprived of office, and the confiscation of all their property to our exchequer.[1]

GRANADA, MARCH 30, 1492
FERDINAND THE CATHOLIC
ISABELLA THE CATHOLIC
KING AND QUEEN OF THE SPAINS
PROMULGATED, APRIL 29, 1492

Immediately after the Edict was officially announced throughout the kingdom, Don Isaac Abravanel and Abraham Seneor raced to Alhambra to bargain for the lives of approximately 300,000 Jews. An expulsion from Spain meant certain death for thousands of Jews because they had so few countries that would accept them. England, France and Germany had expelled the Jews centuries before. Entrenched for so many centuries in Spain, the Jews still did not believe they would really be forced to leave. They felt confident that Abravanel, Seneor, and Melamed would convince the Catholic Monarchs to rescind the edict.

Abravanel, Seneor, and Melamed arrived at Alhambra and were given three chances to meet with the monarchs. Presumably they were working out a compromise that would allow the Jews to remain. Cardinal Mendoza, the marquis of Cadiz, and the duke of Medinaceli also met with the king and queen in an effort to have the edict rescinded. Negotiations were underway to raise a large sum of money to protect the right of the Jews to remain and it looked, for a short time, as though the edict would be repealed.

On their third audience, Abravanel, Seneor, and Melamed arrived at Alhambra and were ushered into the Hall of the Ambassadors, which was once Boabdil's throneroom, with its magnificent mudejar windows, with views of the rolling hills, the olive trees, and the lush farmland of Granada. Don Isaac presented King Ferdinand with 30,000 ducats and an agreement to pay up to 300,000 ducats to have the edict of expulsion rescinded.[2] Ferdinand was prepared to accept the proposal. Now he would have the needed funds to patronize Columbus, and his Jewish subjects, who were his physicians, craftsmen, and scholars, would be allowed to remain. He was most anxious to keep Don Isaac and Seneor. Don Isaac wanted the Catholic Monarchs to understand how devastating an expulsion would be. He beseeched the king and queen to accept the money. A direct descendant of King David, Abravanel spoke of the fire and brimstone that would befall them should they cast out God's chosen people. He confronted them with the hard facts that the Jews had few places to go, reminded them that the Jews had lived in Spain before Christ walked upon the earth, and told them that their expulsion from Spain would mean almost certain death for thousands of innocent people. The Catholic Monarchs were on the verge of rescinding the edict when Tomas Torquemada stormed into the Hall, raised a cross above his head and cried, "Judas Iscariot sold his master for thirty pieces of silver. Your Highness would sell him anew for thirty thousand. Here he is, take him and barter him away."[3] He threw the cross and hit Isabella in the head. Ferdinand stood and exclaimed the edict would stand. Isabella turned to Don Isaac and cried, "The Lord hath put this thing into the heart of the king. . . . The king's heart . . . is in the hands of the Lord, as the rivers of water. He turns it whithersoever He will."[4] Torquemada's timing could not have been more perfect. The La Guardia case still hung like a heavy pall over the Royal Court. Torquemada must have known that a dramatic entrance and interruption of the delicate negotiations could sway Isabella and Ferdinand, as indeed it did. There is little doubt that Isabella allowed the edict to stand because of her religious conviction. Ferdinand's motivation was economic, and with this dramatic interruption, he was given the perfect excuse to let the edict stand. He could hide behind a religious pretext. Although he wished to keep his Jewish treasurers, he knew that with the expulsion, he'd be acquiring more money than Abravanel or Seneor could ever offer. Ferdinand would no longer be pacified with Jewish tributes but would confiscate all Jewish assets. Torquemada had given him the excuse to say no to Abravanel and Seneor. Not the thousands of ducats nor the beseeching of Abravanel or Seneor could stop the expulsion. Abravanel recorded his attempt to stop the expulsion and how it was all in vain:

> I pleaded with the king many times. I supplicated him thus: "Save O king Why do this to thy servants? Lay on us every tribute and ransom gold and silver and everything that the children of Israel possess they shall willingly give to their fatherland." I sought out my friends, those who stood near the king and enjoy his confidence,

and begged them to beseech and petition him to revoke the evil decree concerning our destruction and annihilation, but all in vain. Like an adder which stoppeth its ears, he remained deaf to our appeals. The queen, also, was standing by his side, but she would not listen to our plea. On the contrary, she argued in favor of carrying out the plan. I neither rested nor spared myself, yet the calamity was not averted.[5]

Along with the plan to expel the Jews, the Catholic Monarchs plotted to prevent Abravanel and Seneor from leaving. They devised a plan to kidnap Don Isaac's grandson, hoping that then the family would not emigrate but rather convert and stay. Don Isaac found out about the conspiracy and had the child sent to one of his relatives (probably a sister) in Portugal. The Abravanels were not going to be blackmailed. It was another matter, though, in Abraham Seneor's case. To this day, Seneor is referred to as one who turned from the light because he and his family converted. On June 15, 1492, in the church of Santa Maria de Guadalupe, Abraham Seneor and his family were baptized and took the Christian family name Coronel. The king and queen attended their baptism.[6] In actuality, Seneor had been blackmailed. He was told either to convert and remain in Spain or the Jews would be destroyed. The most tragic part of this event was that most of the Jews considered Seneor a traitor. Baer sheds important light on what happened to the Seneor family when he relates that "the queen had sworn that if Don Abraham Seneor were not baptized, she would destroy all the Jewish communities; he did what he did to save the lives of many people, not of his own desire. His son-in-law also followed his example, for both of them fell victim to the queen's design, they having reared her and made her great."[7] Whereas Seneor was forced to suffer the humiliation of his traitorous act, Abravanel's fate was to lead the Jews out of Spain. Along with other prominent rabbis and congregation leaders, Abravanel helped organize the exodus. They arranged ships to carry their people away and made sure that the price of passage was paid for the poor who could not afford the exorbitant fares. The ships would take the Jews to Africa, Turkey, Portugal, and Italy. Some Jews stole into France. The largest number, approximately 150,000, emigrated to Portugal. The Catholic Monarchs extended the date of expulsion to the end of July but within those three months the Jews had to sell their property and prepare to leave forever. Many Christians took advantage of their plight, offering very little for land and a poor exchange for the assets they were not allowed to take out of Spain. They were not allowed to take coins, gold, silver, or precious gems and found they had to exchange their goods for cloth and animals.

Abravanel believed that this catastrophic disaster was the prelude to the coming of the Messiah and this messianic dream helped give the Jews the strength to begin new lives in strange new lands. Piling their household goods on wagons and on the backs of mules, they closed their homes and took the various roads to the sea. Priests stopped them at every point on their march, begging them to convert, but their conviction that the Messiah was coming and the knowledge of how they would be treated as Conversos gave many of them the will to go on. Very few converted. They had seen how poorly the Old Christians had accepted the Conversos into the society. They had seen what had happened to the Marranos who tried to practice their religion secretly, had witnessed the autos de fé. They rejected the priests and marched on to the ports of Cartagena, Valencia, Cadiz, Laredo, Barcelona and Tarragona. Abravanel and other prominent leaders marched with their brethren to the sea. They lifted the sick and helped the young. They encouraged the women to sing and play their tambourines, for it was a time to rejoice not to mourn; the Messiah was soon coming. Abravanel recorded the sentiment of the march.

> When the Jews learned of the evil that had befallen them, they wept and mourned. Wherever the news of the king's decree was received there was great wailing and lamentation, for no such sorrow had befallen the Jews since they had been driven out of their own land and sent into exile to live among strangers. . . . Everyman said to his brother, "Be strong and of good courage for the sake of our faith and the Law of our God. If He lets us live, we shall live. If, however, we are to die, we shall not be faithless to our covenant. Nor will we falter, but march onward in the name of our God.[8]

They laboriously made their way down the muddy roads, singing as they went, trying to keep their spirits up. And it was everywhere the same, from every province. The Christians watched and were not unmoved. The chronicler Andres Bernaldez, a Spanish priest, recorded:

> Within the terms fixed by the edict of expulsion, the Jews sold and disposed of their property for a mere nothing; they went about asking Christians to buy but found no buyers; fine houses and estates were sold for trifles; a house was exchanged for a mule; and a vineyard given for a little cloth or linen. . . . The rich Jews

paid the expenses of the departure of the poor, practicing toward each other the greatest charity so that, except for a very few of the poorest, they would not become converts. . . . in the first week of July, they took the hardship of the road upon themselves and left the lands of their birth—children and adults, old people and youngster, on foot, and gentlemen mounted on donkeys and other animals, and in carts. And they continued their journeys, each one to the ports to which they had to go, and they went along the roads and through the fields with great travail and misfortune, some falling, others rising, some dying, others being born, others falling ill, that there was no Christian who did not feel sorry for them, and always, through wherever they passed the Jews were invited to be baptized. And some, because of the hardship, converted and remained, but these were very few. The rabbis strengthened their resolve and made the women and young people play on pipes and tambourines to cheer the people, and thus they left Castile and arrived at the ports of the sea . . . Those who were to embark at the port of Cadiz, as soon as they glimpsed the sea, let out loud shouts, men and women, the old and the children. In their prayers they beseeched God for mercy and hoped to see some miracles of God, that he might open a path for them in the sea.[9]

Abravanel was paid a debt from the Crown of 1,500,000 maravedis, some of which had gone to pay for Columbus's initial expenses. The fact that the earliest monies for the voyage came from Abravanel leads one to suspect that Abravanel must have been one of Columbus's most steadfast supporters. With the debt from the Crown repaid, Abravanel was one of the few Jews who was allowed to leave

Spain with money. In the end, King Ferdinand had accomplished his goal and the original 30,000 gold ducats Abravanel and Seneor promised looked like a paltry sum indeed. Netanyahu estimates that over 7,000,000 maravedis were collected after the expulsion of the Jews in one city alone.[10] Ferdinand no longer had to ask for loans in order to finance Columbus. He also would not have to share the profits or the glory. But what King Ferdinand did not seem to realize was his loss of one of his most precious natural resources in the bargain, the Jews of Spain. While Spain was now about to enter an unprecedented time of glory and wealth as a direct result of Columbus's historic voyage, she would sorely miss the colorful, varied ethnic influences that both the Jews and Moslems had offered Spain over the preceding centuries. In an exchange for complete unification between Church and State, Spain lost many of her great scientists, doctors, lawyers, poets, teachers, and skilled craftsmen. On August 2, 1492, the ninth of Av, the anniversary of the destruction of the Temple in Jerusalem, the Jews converged upon the different Spanish ports. It was considered to be an ill omen to begin a trip or new enterprise on that day. Columbus had originally planned to set sail on August second but changed his date to the third. His official reason was the overcrowding of the ports because of the Jewish exodus. Many scholars believe, however, that Columbus was well aware that August second was the ninth of Av and that he would not begin his voyage on that ill-fated date for the Jews.

10

VOYAGES
OUT TO SEA

1492

Columbus taking leave of Ferdinand and Isabella at the port of Palos in 1492. From Theodore de Bry.

Look, they move! No comrades near but curses;
Tears gleam in beards of men sore with reverses;
Flowers from the fields abandoned, loving nurses;
Fondly deck the women's raven hair.

Faded, scentless flowers that shall remind them
Of their precious homes and graves behind them;
Old men, clasping Torah-scrolls, unbind them,
Lift the parchment flags, and silent lead.

"Mock not thy light, O sun, our morrow,
Cease not, cease not, O ye songs of sorrow!
From what land a refuge can we borrow,
Weary, thrust-out, God-forsaken we?

"Where, oh! where is rest for thy long-hated,
Hunted folk, whose fate in death unsated?
Oh! where is God?" So swelled the wail unbated,
From the mountains down unto the sea.

Could ye, suff'ring souls, peer through the Future,
From despair ye would awake to rapture:
Lo! The Genoese boldly steers to capture
Freedom's realm beyond an unsailed sea!

—Ludwig August Frankl, Stuttgart, 1836[1]

W hen the Jews arrived at the Spanish ports and beheld the water, the devastating impact of the edict took hold. Men wept, and women pulled their hair as they cried. Some took fists full of earth to carry with them, while others clutched flowers and small mementos of their life in Spain. The ships that had been hastily arranged were hardly seaworthy carracks, and the price of passage was enormous. Rats and roaches scurried unchecked, spreading disease. The Italian republics of Venice, Genoa, Florence, Lucca, and Siena, as well as the duchies of Savoy, Milan, Modena, and Ferrara had very severe restrictions for their own Jewish population and had closed their ports to the Spanish Jews known as Sephardim.[2] Don Isaac Abravanel and his family, on board one of nine ships heading

east, finally found a welcoming harbor in Naples about one
month later. They were quarantined, however, because a
number of passengers had contracted the plague. The Jews
were in such distress when they arrived that a witness recorded, "One might have taken them for spectres, so ema-
ciated were they, so cadaverous in their aspect, and with
eyes so sunken; they differed in nothing from the dead,
except in the power of motion, which indeed they scarcely
retained."[3] The scene was much the same at the ports in
Turkey and North Africa where approximately 150,000 Jews
found refuge. The sultan, Bayazet II, graciously accepted the
Jews and "issued a proclamation in the European provinces
of his empire that the Jews must be received with the utmost
hospitality, and threatened with death any one who would
mistreat or oppress them."[4] The Turkish Jews opened their
arms to their brethren sailing from Spain. Jews also found
safe havens in Corfu and on smaller Greek islands. Of the
150,000 Jews who fled to Portugal, a tax of one hundred
crusados was levied on every Jew and only 600 Jewish
families were permitted to stay.[5] But as Professor H. Graetz
notes, the Jews in Portugal did not fare well. "The balance
were to remain in the country only eight months. Those who
would be found in the country after the expiration . . . or
those who could show no receipt for their capitation tax,
were to be reduced to slavery."[6] The total number of Jews
expelled from Spain in 1492 ranged between 300,000 and
500,000 people. Slavery, starvation, disease, and despair
were their companions. The voyages of the Jews became the
very antithesis of the glorious, historic voyage that was
launched one day later.

If Columbus had slept at all on the night of August 2, he
rose before the dawn broke to the quiet sounds of water

slapping against the rigged ships and the occasional call of a gull. The anguished cries of the Jews boarding ships had ended. But the events from the day before must have haunted him. No Christian was untouched by the wrenching scenes of the Jews herded onto the ships. The smell of tar and wet hemp rope filled the air. Before dawn, on August 3, the sails were raised, and Columbus's ships slid away from their anchorage.

* * *

Did Columbus harbor any doubts concerning his ability to bring the three ships and their crews safely home again? It seems he did not but, rather, was very confident he would find land after a short crossing of the Ocean Sea. One can almost sense, five hundred years later, the excitement he must have felt on August 3, 1492. We can imagine the scene as the crew heaved and sang as the sails were unfurled with large red crosses and royal crests of the castle and the lion billowing out against the early morning sky. The sails caught the breezes that blew the ships down the river of Saltes, then dropped out of sight as the ships headed for the Ocean Sea.

With the expulsion of the Jews occurring the previous day, one might wonder if Columbus harbored a secret desire to discover a land where the Jews could live in peace. Simon Wiesenthal argues that Columbus indeed had a hidden agenda, a secret mission to find such a haven for the Jews.[7] But if Columbus did, he kept it buried deep within his heart.

Though King Ferdinand and Queen Isabella had ordered the city of Palos to provide Columbus with three sturdy caravels, the enterprise would have been next to impossible to put together without the support of Martin Alonso Pinzon and his brothers Vicente Yanez Pinzon and

Francisco Martin Pinzon. In 1492, sailors believed the Ocean Sea was infested with sea monsters, and that the westerly winds would make it impossible for them to return. Columbus was a foreigner in Palos and would never have been able to convince them otherwise. The Pinzon brothers, however, were respected sea captains from Palos, knew the local sailors, and were able to muster enough men to gather three full crews. Martin Alonso was the captain of the *Pinta* and his younger brother, Vicente, commanded the *Nina*. Columbus took command of the flagship, the *Santa Maria*.

Martin Pinzon was a fascinating character, who, but for lack of persistence, missed having his name emblazoned in history as the discoverer of the New World. It seems that Pinzon also knew that there was a westerly ocean route to the East. He had traveled to Rome as a young man (long before Columbus arrived in Spain), and in the Vatican Library had seen a Hebraic document concerning a western ocean voyage made during the time of the Queen of Sheba and King Solomon. The document recorded a trip to Japan made by someone crossing the sea from the queen's Court.[8] Pinzon also dreamed of sailing west to reach the East. But once Columbus obtained the royal backing from King Ferdinand and Queen Isabella, Pinzon threw all his efforts into helping Columbus. Did Pinzon hope to seize all the glory by sailing faster than Columbus and returning home first? It is interesting to note that Pinzon commanded the faster vessel, the *Pinta*. Columbus's flagship, the *Santa Maria*, was not as seaworthy. Shortly after the initial crossing, Martin Pinzon sailed away from the flagship, looking for Japan. Though he joined up again with Columbus before they sailed home, Columbus greatly feared that Pinzon would beat him back to Spain and claim the discoveries as his own.

The *Santa Maria* had been chartered from Juan de la Cosa of Santona, a town located in the north of Spain on the Bay of Biscay. The *Santa Maria* had been called *La Gallega* or *Marigalante* (*Frivolous Mary*), but Columbus felt the *Frivolous Mary* was not a suitable name for a ship about to make history so he rechristened her the *Santa Maria*. While the *Nina* and the *Pinta* were smaller, faster caravels, the *Santa Maria* was a carrack, a chunkier ship, sitting low in the water. It seems that Columbus was angry with the town of Palos because the king and queen had ordered them to provide him with a ship well suited for exploration, and the heavy *Santa Maria* was not well suited for his purposes. However, the two sleeker three-masted caravels, the *Nina* and the *Pinta*, were well suited for this voyage. The caravels differed, at first, in their rigging. The *Nina's* rigging was changed from lateen to square rig when the expedition reached the Canary Islands. The effort it took to pull the mainsail completely around the mast proved too awkward for the long voyage ahead. The square rigged sails just had to be trimmed and were better suited for the dangerous open sea.

There were three men from the Nino family on the first voyage. The *Nina* was owned by Juan Nino from the town of Moguer, not far from Palos. Peralonso Nino was Columbus's pilot on the *Santa Maria*. The third brother, Francisco, who was only nineteen years old in 1492, sailed again as Columbus's pilot on the second and fourth voyages. Columbus trusted the Nino family far more than the Pinzons.[9]

Most of the crew were well-seasoned sailors from the towns of Palos, Moguer, Huelva, Lepe and as far away as Cadiz, Seville, Cordova, Jeres and Puerto Santa Maria.[10] All the men on board were Christian, but a number were Conversos, some of whom had been baptized only days before the ships set sail.

The most famous of the Conversos was Luis de Torres. Columbus had hired him as an interpreter because he suspected that when they reached the lands of Khan, they would find some of the lost tribes of Israel. Columbus hoped Torres would be able to communicate with them in Hebrew. Torres also spoke Arabic. Another Converso on the voyage was Alonso de la Calle, his name originating from the street, Jew's Lane. The surgeon, Marco, and the physician Mestre Bernal were also of Jewish descent. Bernal came from Tortosa, a city in Catalonia. He had walked as a penitent in Valencia in 1490, and had witnessed his wife, Isabel, die at the stake, one year after the Colom family had died in the auto de fé in Tarragona, Catalonia.[11] It is interesting to note that some of these Conversos were from Catalonia, just as Columbus's family might have been.

The comptroller and agent for the Crown, Rodrigo Sanchez de Segovia, was also a Converso who was related to Gabriel Sanchez. As noted, the Sanchez family had members who walked as penitents in autos de fé, and they, too, had lost loved ones at the stake. The brutal Inquisition had touched the lives of most of the Conversos on the voyage, and it appears that Columbus's most trusted men were the Conversos.

Columbus did not have a priest accompany them on the first voyage. Some scholars suggest that this is added proof that he was not a Catholic at heart. After all, one of the intentions of the voyage was to discover new souls to convert, yet no priest's name appears on any of the lists. Priests did accompany Columbus on other voyages but not on the first.

On the voyage to the Canary Islands, Columbus began his famous Journal with this letter.

IN THE NAME OF OUR LORD JESUS CHRIST

Because, most Christian and very exalted excellent and mighty Princes, King and Queen of the Spains and of the islands in the Sea, our Lord and Lady, in this present year 1492, after Your Highnesses had made an end to the war with the Moors who ruled in Europe, and had concluded the war in the very great city of Granada, where in the present year, of the second day of the month of January, by force of arms I saw the royal standards of Your Highnesses placed on the towers of Alhambra (which is the citadel of the said city), and I saw the Moorish King come forth to the gates of the city and kiss the royal hands of Your Highnesses and of the Prince my lord, and soon after in that same month, through the information that I had given to Your Highnesses concerning the lands of India, and of a prince who is called "Grand Khan" which is to say in our vernacular "King of Kings," how many times he and his ancestors had sent to Rome to seek doctors in our Holy Faith to instruct him therein, and that never had the Holy Father provided them, and thus were lost many people through lapsing into idolatries and receiving doctrines of perdition;

AND Your Highnesses, as Catholic Christians and Princes devoted to the Holy Christian Faith and the propagators thereof, and enemies of the sect of Mahomet and of all idolatries and heresies, resolved to send me Christopher Columbus to the said regions of India, to see the said princes and peoples and lands and (to observe) the disposition of them and of all, and the manner in which may be undertaken their conversion to our Holy Faith, and ordained that I should not go by

land (the usual way) to the Orient, but by route of the
Occident, by which no one to this day knows for sure
that anyone has gone;—

THEREFORE, after all the Jews had been exiled
from your realms and dominions, in the same month of
January Your Highnesses commanded me that with a
sufficient fleet I should go to the said regions of India,
and for this granted me many rewards, and ennobled
me so that henceforth I might call myself by the noble
title and be Admiral-in-Chief of the Ocean Sea and
Viceroy and Perpetual Governor of all the islands and
mainlands that I should discover and win, or that henceforth might be discovered and won in the Ocean Sea,
and that my eldest son should succeed me, and thus
from rank to rank for ever.[12]

The letter goes on to describe his journey from Granada to
Palos and then to the Canary Islands. It was a dangerous and
significant omission on his part not to praise the Catholic
Monarchs for the expulsion of the Jews. He ran a great risk
of offending them by not offering the expected flattery and
praise for their action.

Fortuitously, Columbus sighted the Grand Canary Island on August 9, because the *Pinta's* helm suddenly
snapped, and she limped into port. Columbus immediately
tried to replace the ship but after a full month of searching
for another vessel, he returned to find that the *Pinta* was
repaired. Finally on September 9 they were ready to sail
westward, to venture into the unknown world of the Ocean
Sea. Columbus's years of mapping trade winds and of gathering information and experience would be of critical importance in the enterprise's success. Where Estreito and Dulmo
failed, Columbus was destined to succeed.

In the first few days out, his writings reflect his unflagging faith in the scheme but as the days rolled along, his anxiety increased. He began to keep two sets of records, one for the men, the second set for himself. As the length of the ocean seemed to grow, the words of Mestre Joseph Vizinho and Mestre Rodrigo, of Fray Hernando Talavera, Abraham Zacuto and the commission in Salamanca, all of whom insisted that the ocean was much larger than he had calculated, must have intimidated him. The crew, ever restless, panicked because of the constant westerlies. When a terrible storm blew up sending the ships in every direction, the men were relieved to see the winds change. Columbus, too, felt tremendous relief that his theories proved correct. The winds shifted enough so that they would eventually be able to tack back east. After the storm Columbus wrote that a miracle had taken place, and that he had been saved just as Moses had been saved by the parting of the sea.

However, his travails were just beginning. A few days later they sailed into a great meadow of sea grass known as the Sargasso Sea. This, too, created panic among the crew. Another troubling event was the shifting of the compass needle away from Polaris, the north star by which Columbus charted his course due west. But Columbus's gravest doubts began when the enterprise crossed the sixty-fifth meridian of longitude on October 6, long after he had estimated landfall. Still they had not sighted land. He knew that according to his own calculations they had gone too far, and that their supplies would not last the trip back without replenishing them. The most important meeting of the enterprise occurred when he and Martin Pinzon agreed to sail only three or four more days before turning around! By October 10, four days later, there were many signs that they were very close to land. Branches floated in the water and flocks of birds were flying westward. They traveled on.

An interesting story accompanies the first sighting of land on October 12, 1492. Columbus thought that he saw land at 10 P.M. on October 11, but was unsure and did not cry out. At 2 A.M. on October 12, Rodrigo de Triana, standing on the forecastle of the *Pinta*, sighted San Salvador or Guanahani (more recent research has pointed to the island of Samana Cay as the original sighting), and he cried, "Land, land!" A new world was discovered by the Europeans.

When Triana cried, "land," some say the words he used were, "I, I," Hebrew for, "Island, Island." He was calling to a Converso on board ship who supposedly answered in Hebrew, "W'annah" (and where?), to which Triana answered, "Hen-i" (there is the island). This unusual story claims that the words "W'annah . . . Hen-i" were the origin of the name Uanaheni or Guanahani.[13] Kayserling dismisses the story because the word *Guanahani* also was found in the native language. However, this does not negate the possibility that Triana may have been a Converso. Cecil Roth suggested that he was.[14] The story concerning Triana goes on to note that Columbus defrauded him of 10,000 maravedis and a waistcoat promised by the king and queen to the first man who sighted land. Columbus claimed that he had seen land on the evening of October 11. Incensed at being cheated out of his reward, Triana left Spain and sailed to Africa where he renounced his Christianity for his old faith.[15] No one, unfortunately, has been able to prove that his old faith was Judaism. These tales, however, lead to the belief that there were a number of undocumented Conversos on board the three ships. The timing of Columbus's departure and the expulsion was so close that there probably were a number of converted Jews who signed on board. Columbus may or may not have had a secret mission to find a kingdom where Jews would be able to live in peace but certainly the Conversos must have held on to that dream. The Conversos or Marranos on board must have hoped that they would indeed find a land where they could practice their religion away from the eyes of the Inquisition. Although new land was discovered and Marranos flocked to the New World, they would not be free, unfortunately, from the tribunals and fires of the Spanish Inquisition.

11

THE SPANIARDS DISCOVER A NEW WORLD

1492

Columbus lands on Hispaniola. From Theodore de Bry.

When dawn broke on October 12, 1492, Columbus, Torres, Martin and Vicente Pinzon, Rodrigo Sanchez, and a few others climbed into small boats and rowed ashore to greet the naked men who had gathered there. Overwhelmed with the miracle of dry land, the Spaniards climbed out of their boats, waded through the warm salt water, then fell to their knees and kissed the ground. The native people were completely awed by the spectacle of three ships and the strange men. They thought the Spaniards were "men from Heaven." Columbus planted the royal banners firmly in the sandy soil, claiming the land for King Ferdinand and Queen Isabella. The other Spaniards doffed their feathered hats and bowed before him, pledging their allegiance to the new Admiral of the Ocean Sea. Unknowingly, they had arrived in a New World. Their discovery would bring glory to Spain, pain and suffering to the indigenous population.

Though the biographer, Las Casas, was not with Columbus on the first voyage, his account of the historic landing gives insight to the Spanish perception of the event.

> Presently they saw naked people, and the Admiral went ashore in the armed ship's boat with the royal standard displayed. So did the captains of the *Pinta* and *Niña*, Martín Alonso Pinzón and Vicente Yáñez his brother, in their boats, with the banners of the Expedition, on which were depicted a green cross with an F on one arm and a Y on the other, and over each his or her crown. And, all having rendered thanks to Our Lord kneeling on the ground, embracing it with tears of joy for the immeasurable mercy of having reached it, the Admiral arose and gave this island the name *San Salvador*. Thereupon he summoned to him the two captains, Rodrigo de Escobedo secretary of the armada and Rodrigo Sánchez of Segovia, and all others who came ashore, as witnesses; and in the presence of many natives of that land assembled together, took possession of that island in the name of the Catholic Sovereigns with appropriate words and ceremony. . . . Forthwith the Christians hailed him as Admiral and Viceroy and swore to obey him as one who represented Their Highnesses. . . . Many Indians having come together for that ceremony and rejoicing, the Admiral, seeing that they were a gentle and peaceful people and of great simplicity, gave them some little red caps and glass beads which they hung around their necks, and other things of slight worth, which they all valued at the highest prices.[1]

This was Columbus's first encounter with the native Taino culture, the Arawak language group of people, who lived in the Bahamas in 1492. In Columbus's own words he describes the Arawak people.

> In order that we might win good friendship, because I knew that they were a people who could better be freed and converted to our Holy Faith by love than by force, I gave to some of them red caps and to some glass beads, which they hung on their necks and many other things of slight value, in which they took much pleasure; they remained so much our friends that it was a marvel . . . Saturday October 13: At daybreak there came to the beach many of these men, all young men as I have said, and all of good stature, very handsome people . . . They are so ingenuous and free with all they have, that no one would believe it who has not seen it; of anything that they possess, if it be asked of them, they never say no; on the contrary, they invite you to share it and show as much love as if their hearts went with it.[2]

The Arawaks had developed an agrarian society, cultivating corn and yams and making their cassava bread from the yucca plant. They had a range of crafts including pottery, shell jewelry making, and cotton spinning. Columbus was amazed by the Arawaks' sense of humanity, which he interpreted as weakness and tragically exploited. However, the first encounters were friendly and full of good will. The Arawaks were delighted with the trinkets and in several villages Columbus was thought to be a god. From island to island news spread quickly that "men from heaven" had arrived but several caciques or chiefs were justifiably skeptical. One of the natives who had been captured by Columbus escaped and informed the others that he had been imprisoned. Concerning this incident Morison notes, "Perhaps the released canoeman had given them the tip that 'men from Heaven,' were more cheerful receivers than givers."[3] Luis de Torres tried to communicate in Hebrew with the Arawaks but had no success.

Columbus coerced several Arawaks to live on board the *Santa Maria* where he tried to teach them Castilian. The one most successful Arawak was eventually baptized and given the Christian name Diego Colon. His services were invaluable to Columbus since he served as his loyal interpreter. Diego learned that the Spaniards were seeking gold, a metal of little value to them. Diego explained to his people that the Spaniards were searching for the land of Khan, which was interpreted as the land of gold. Morison notes that "by now the captive guides had grasped that gold was what the men from Heaven were after. . . . Having observed the Christians taking specimens of plants and going over everything in the native houses in search of gold, the simple savages perhaps thought that they were collecting leaves, earthenware and hammocks, of which there were plenty everywhere."[4] After much island hopping, Diego gleaned from the various tribes that there was gold in Cuba. Columbus was certain that Cuba was the mainland, Cathay, which he so ardently sought. By October 28, they had reached Cuba. He wrote, "It is certain that this is the mainland, and that I am near to Quinsay [the imperial city of Cathay], one hundred leagues more or less."[5] Columbus took the word *Cubanacan* for Kubla Khan, so that as he skirted the island's shoreline, he expected to see the gold-tiled roofs described by Marco Polo rise before him, but, of course, the golden roofs did not materialize. Instead, Columbus had come upon a fertile land full of flora and fauna he had never seen before. Parrots and iguanas, along with cinnamon, pepper, and strange new spices were brought to him by the people trying to please the "men from heaven." While Columbus made note of the lush vegetation and the beauty of the land, he was not pleased. They had not yet found gold.

Columbus guessed that Cathay was further inland and sent Luis de Torres along with Rodrigo de Jerez on an expedition to find the fabulous city. It was at this point that without the consent of Columbus, Martin Pinzon sailed away from the two other ships and began his own quest for Cipango.

Angered by Pinzon's mutiny and disappointed in Torres's failure to find Cathay, Columbus pressed on to Bohio (Haiti). He took great delight in the beautiful island of mahogany and palms, of lobsters and colorful tropical fish, but still the gold he so desperately needed to justify the entire expedition was not found. Comparing Haiti to Castile, he wrote to Ferdinand and Isabella, "This island and all others are as much yours as Castile. The people have no weapons and go naked and have no spirit for warfare. They are very cowardly and one thousand of them would not stand up to three [of us]. The result is that they are suitable for discipline and to be made to work, to sow and do everything, to build towns and to learn to be dressed and adopt our ways."[6] There was no doubt that he was the conqueror prepared to enslave the Arawak people.

This brave new world that Columbus stumbled onto was no paradise. Carib natives, living just south in the Caribbean Islands, often made warfare on their gentle Arawak neighbors. The cannibalistic Caribs terrorized the Arawaks by capturing members of their tribe and then devouring them. Some of the Arawak people thought that the Spaniards were Caribs but, tragically, the Spaniards would become the more deadly enemy. As a result of new diseases carried over from Europe, of hard labor, and slavery instigated by the Spaniards, the Bahama Arawaks were annihilated within a few short years after the discovery.

Las Casas first championed the cause of the Arawaks when he arrived in 1500, challenging Columbus on the policy of slavery that the latter initiated. Though one cannot condone Columbus's policy, he was duplicating the Portuguese practice of slavery that was in place when he sailed to Africa. Slavery was still a common practice throughout the Mediterranean countries. White slave trade, usually involving prisoners of war impressed by conquering armies, was not unusual. The scholar Prescott records that during the reconquista Ferdinand and Isabella freed many Christian slaves from the Moors. When Boabdil surrendered Alhambra to Ferdinand and Isabella, his negotiated treaty assured the remaining Moors that they would not be pressed into slavery.[7] Queen Isabella abhorred Columbus's practice of enslaving the Bahama Arawak population. But the queen's policy was duplicitous, for slavery was condoned if the Arawaks had been taken in battle. The monarchs' position on slavery is noted by Madariaga.

> According to the Admiral's report, these Indians had been taken in battle and, in the light of the ethics of the times, they were fair prey for slavery. After the fall of Málaga—the one case in which the King and Queen had met with stubborn resistance and a rejection of all offers

of good treatment on surrender—slaves were freely
taken from the Moorish population. Pope Innocent VIII
received one hundred Moors "well harnessed" and
Queen Isabel sent thirty maids, "the most beautiful that
could be found," to her cousin, the Queen of Naples,
and thirty to the Queen of Portugal. Presents of slaves
were given to a number of grandees and Court dignitar-
ies, the list being headed by the Cardinal of Spain who
received one hundred and twenty.[8]

Though he enslaved a few Arawaks on the first voyage,
Columbus made slavery a major objective for the other three
expeditions. On the second voyage alone, Columbus enslaved over five hundred people and sent them to Spain.

* * *

Just as the native Bahama population and Moorish
population were enslaved, so too were the Jews. In 1492,
many of the expelled Jews were sold by the unscrupulous
sea captains who had accepted exorbitant prices for their
"safe" passage. But wherever Jews were held as slaves, the
local Jewish populations responded quickly to free their
brethren. Rabbi Moses Kapsali, living in Turkey in 1492,
raised money to free many of the Jews who had been sold
into slavery in that country. The same was true of Elkanah
Kapsali in Crete.[9] He, too, paid a high ransom for Jews who
had been sold into slavery. Graetz writes:

Moses Kapsali was indefatigable in his acts of benevo-
lence toward the Spanish exiles who reached Turkey as
beggars or slaves. He traveled from community to community, and imposed a special tax upon the wealthy

Jews for the redemption of the Spanish captives. He
had no occasion to employ force, either, for the Turkish
Jews contributed gladly to the relief of the victims of
Christian fanaticism.[10]

The North African Jews were not in as secure a position as
those in Turkey but they too did what they could for the
Sephardim who landed enslaved on their shore. Dr. Jacob
Marcus notes that many Jews died before relief could reach
them.

Many of the exiled Spaniards went to [North African]
countries, to Fez, Tlemcen, and the Berber provinces,
under the King of Tunis. These North African lands are
across the Mediterranean from Spain. On account of
their large numbers the Moors did not allow them into
their cities, and many of them died in the fields from
hunger, thirst and lack of everything. The lions and
bears, which are numerous in this country, killed some
of them while they lay starving outside the cities.[11]

But here too, the local Jewish leadership responded. "A Jew
in the kingdom of Tlemcen, named Abraham, the viceroy
who ruled the kingdom, made part of them come to this
kingdom, and he spent a large amount of money to help
them."[12] Small clusters of Sephardim were rescued from
slavery and resettled around the Mediterranean lands where
Jewish populations preexisted.

The fate of the Jews in Portugal went from bad to worse
to catastrophic. Their situation worsened shortly after their

arrival when King Joao enslaved those Jews who did not have the tax money for the right to remain in Portugal. Marcus notes that "all Spanish Jews, who were still in Portugal in 1493, were enslaved by King John (1481–1495). The children were sent to the isle of St. Thomas, off the coast of Africa."[13] But the entire Jewish population was in jeopardy when in 1496 the new Portuguese king, Manuel, married Queen Isabella's daughter, Isabella. As part of the nuptial agreement, Manuel assured Queen Isabella that all the Jews would be expelled from Portugal just as they had been from Spain. In April of 1497, Manuel issued an order that all Jewish children be baptized, separated from their parents, and raised in Catholic homes. Many parents converted in order to keep their children but it was to no avail, for the children were taken from them anyway. King Manuel issued an edict to enslave all the Jews who remained in Portugal and then went on to obstruct their efforts to leave as they had been allowed to do in Spain. Graetz states that King Manuel

> placed so many obstacles in the way of their embarkation that they could not leave before the month of October, when all who were still found on Portuguese soil were to lose their lives or at least their liberty. Thereupon the king shut all the Jews in an open square, like cattle in a pen, declared them his slaves, and gave them the choice between voluntary acceptance of Christianity, in which case they would receive honors and wealth, and forcible baptism.[14]

Some experts estimate that only 10 percent of the 500,000 Jews survived the expulsions from Spain and Portugal and those few who did survive were only able to do so with the help of their brethren. The Bahama Arawak people, however, did not have a network of brethren to save even a small number of their people.

But the slave trade was not Columbus's main objective on the first expedition. He was clearly searching for Cathay and Cipango, hoping to find gold. While in Haiti, Columbus heard about a great gold mine in a land called Cibao (Hispaniola), and he was sure that this island must truly be Cipango. He sailed to Cibao, thinking it was a separate island but actually it was all part of Hispaniola. He laid anchor on December 24. In the middle of the night, the tides changed, and the *Santa Maria* ran upon a reef. Attempts were made to save the ship but they were futile. At night the men transferred to the *Nina*, abandoning the *Santa Maria*. A native chief, Guacanagari, provided the invaluable service of rescuing the men from the ship and transferring supplies to shore. The *Nina* could not accommodate the *Santa Maria's* crew, and so Columbus was forced to establish a colony called Villa de la Navidad. He saw the shipwreck as divine intervention and wrote, "The Lord had ordained this shipwreck so that he might choose this place for a settlement. . . . Without this I would not have been able to leave people here, nor to provide them with so much equipment, weapons and supplies."[15] As the Spaniards began to build a fort, they noticed the native people wore small amounts of gold. Columbus was certain that the fabulous mines of the Grand Khan were just inland from their new settlement. He directed volunteers from the crew of the *Santa Maria* to finish the fortifications and then to search for the gold mines. He wrote to the king and queen,

In this Espanola, in the situation most convenient and in the best position for the mines of gold and for all communication with the mainland here as well as that there, belonging to the Great Khan, where there will be trade and gain, I have taken possession of a large town. To it I have given the name of La Navidad. Here I have constructed a fort which by now will be furnished, and I have left sufficient men and arms and provisions for more than a year and a ship's boat together with a master craftsman to build others.[16]

He had no fear for the town's safety since the chief, Guacanagari, had proven himself a trusted friend. After all, Guacanagari was the chief of a docile, friendly people.

News of the shipwreck had reached Martin Pinzon. He rejoined Columbus, who was justifiably outraged. At about this same time, some of Columbus's men discovered gold on the Yaque de Norte River and reports of more gold in Yamaye (Jamaica) gave Columbus what he needed to justify the expedition. On January 6, 1493, the Nina and Pinta left the Indies and after a few stops, headed on an easterly course for home. They were returning in winter seas, but miraculously the ships did not shatter in the raging gales. When the Nina and Pinta were separated in a storm on February 13, Columbus feared that Pinzon would arrive in Spain before him and lay claim to all the discoveries. But the Nina was so battered that Columbus could sail no further. On March 4, 1493, Columbus was forced to bring her into King Joao's Lisbon port.

12

THE GOVERNOR

1493–1500

Spaniards attacking an Indian village. From Theodore de Bry.

Columbus was received by King Joao in Lisbon on March 9, 1493. The king appreciated the magnitude of what Columbus had accomplished and honored his new title of Admiral, but from the moment Columbus landed back on European soil, he began to make enemies. He boasted to Joao that he had found much greater wealth than he actually had discovered. He practically taunted the king, who was sincerely grieved that he had not sponsored him. Joao's men were so indignant with his boasting that they plotted to kill him. Quickly realizing that he had angered the Portuguese Court, Columbus hurriedly left Lisbon for Spain. He arrived in Palos to a hero's welcome on March 15. Martin Pinzon sailed into Bayona (a port in Northern Spain) on the same day.

On March 31, 1493, Columbus headed a procession of Arawak people and his men who carried gold, popinjay birds, parrots, gold masks, pearls, and tropical fruit, and proudly marched to Seville.[1] Men, women and children from every local village jammed the dirt road to see the Great Admiral of the Ocean Sea. Madariaga suggests that Columbus might have made this triumphant procession in tribute to the Jews who had marched to the sea just one year before. Madariaga writes, "His triumphant progress through Castille and Aragon was a fit commemoration of the dismal progress of the expelled Jews. He can hardly have failed to think of it while he passed through the same roads and was acclaimed by the same people who one year earlier had watched the tragic exodus in sullen, sad or charitable silence."[2] Columbus was received by Queen Isabella and King Ferdinand, who was recovering from an assassination attempt. Columbus proceeded to tell them of his dangerous voyage, of the encounters with the native people, of the fertile land, of the gold mines, and of how close he was to finding the Grand Khan. He reassured the Catholic Monarchs that on his next voyage he would find Cathay. The queen's choir sang "Te Deum Laudamus," and the monarchs, overwhelmed with all Columbus told them, fell on their knees before him.[3] Columbus was received as royalty, even given the honor of riding beside King Ferdinand. He was received also by Cardinal Mendoza and had his food tested for poison (the mark of a truly important man). On May 28 he was formally granted all the rights and privileges granted to him in the Capitulations of Santa Fe.

Preparations for the second voyage were ordered immediately. Ferdinand and Isabella commanded Don Juan de Fonseca, the Archdeacon of Seville, to organize an army and seventeen vessels for the expedition. Juan de Soria was appointed the chief comptroller, and Francisco Pinelo was appointed treasurer. Together they hired the vessels that were to carry over a thousand men, including crew, soldiers, and settlers. The Catholic Monarchs made it clear to Columbus that this was to be a twofold enterprise. First, he was to establish colonies, and second, he was to see to the conversion of the native people. Fray Bernardo Buil (from Catalan) and a number of other friars accompanied Columbus on this voyage in order to convert the native people. Animal husbandry and farming were to be the main thrust of the expedition; mining gold was of secondary importance. On September 25, 1493, in the port of Cadiz, Columbus gave the order to raise the sails and the enormous expedition departed.

It took six weeks to cross the Atlantic but when the Spaniards arrived back at La Navidad on the evening of November 27 a foreboding silence surrounded the fort. The following day they were met by some of the native people. They told them the Cacique, Guacanagari, had been wounded in an effort to fight off the Caribs who slaughtered all the Spaniards of La Navidad. Upon visiting Guacanagari, Columbus discovered the Cacique was not wounded, and realized it was the local people who had attacked the fort. It seems that over the long months of waiting for Columbus to return, the Spaniards at the fort had antagonized the Arawaks by capturing and raping the women. A strict governor would have dealt with the serious situation immediately but Columbus procrastinated. Instead of implementing a quick, firm course of action concerning Guacanagari, Columbus sailed north in search of gold. To Columbus's great humiliation, Guacanagari escaped. Columbus' servile friend had now become his enemy. Columbus felt that Guacanagari had humiliated him, and that he had been too lenient. After this incident Columbus became brutal in his dealings with native rebellions.

Columbus made four voyages to the new world, proving himself to be an excellent navigator, and a superb cartographer, but a disastrously incompetent governor. He explored the major islands of Cuba, Haiti, Hispaniola, Puerto Rico, Jamaica, Trinidad, many of the lesser islands of the Bahamas and the Caribbean, and some of South America's shoreline, which is now Venezuela. The charts he made were exacting and sophisticated. Columbus belonged at sea with the wind at his back and the high waves before him. At sea he was in all his glory. On land, however, as a governor, his policies were inconsistent, particularly in regard to the native people. With his own men, he was sometimes too lax while at other times he was cruel.

Columbus's search for gold was unsuccessful but he did organize the first town in the New World, Isabela, on the northern coast of Hispaniola. When construction was well underway, Columbus sent Antonio de Torres back to Cadiz, Spain. Gold had been discovered, and Torres carried with him 30,000 ducats of gold, cinnamon, ginger, pepper, wood, parrots, falcons, and twenty-six native people. Columbus requested in return salted meat, wheat, wine, oil, vinegar, sugar, molasses, medicines, almonds, raisins, honey, and rice.[4] But in Isabela, Hispaniola, there was a growing sense of mistrust between Columbus and his men.

Columbus's troubles began to mount when Alonso de Hojeda discovered gold on the island of Cibao (Cuba) and was convinced that Cuba was Cipango. Columbus hurried off with an army, leaving his younger brother, Diego, in charge of Isabela. They did find gold but still Cipango eluded him. However, when Columbus returned to Isabela, he found his brother had no control over the colony he had left behind. There was not enough food. Fray Buil refused his religious services to Columbus because he felt Columbus was too strict with the men (Columbus had several men whipped and hanged for insubordination). In retaliation, Columbus stopped Fray Buil's food supply. Mosen Pedro Margarite tried to bring the two men together but eventually sided with Fray Buil against Columbus. During this time Hojeda subdued the tribe of Caonabo and sent several captive warriors to Columbus. In a rash act, Columbus had the warriors beheaded. Fray Buil was outraged both by Columbus's poor administration and his unusually cruel treatment of his men and the native people. Fray Buil sailed back to Spain on one of the caravels that had arrived with Columbus's brother, Bartholomew. Columbus's trust in Antonio de Torres was not misplaced, for Torres returned with much-needed supplies. Columbus now worried that Fray Buil and Margarite would present a bleak picture of the new settlement to the king and queen, and he sent the ever-faithful Torres back to Spain to defend him. Torres left with five hundred slaves on board the ships.

Fray Buil did condemn Columbus before the Royal Court. Ferdinand and Isabella were so concerned with the way in which Columbus was governing the new settlement that they sent Juan de Aguado to Isabela with instructions to report directly to them. When Aguado arrived in Isabela, Columbus realized he must return immediately to Spain to defend himself. He appointed Bartholomew as Governor, Diego his second, and Francisco Roldan as Alcalde Mayor.

Being at odds with Fray Buil put Columbus in a delicate

position, particularly if he had something in his background to hide. Upon arriving in Cadiz, he donned the robes of a Franciscan monk and presented himself at court in this most humble, religious attire, a far cry from the grand coat he wore on his first homecoming. Madariaga suggests that his humble dress was significant. He writes, "He knew he would be deeply humiliated; so he deliberately humbled himself. . . . says Las Casas, 'he dressed in brown cloth, and I saw him in Seville, when he came back then, dressed almost like a friar of St. Francis.'"5 Madariaga goes on to suggest that there were deeper motives for this action of humility. "The first was a 'mimetic' instinct. . . . He was in outward danger—the displeasure of the Court; what better garb than that of a Franciscan? The second was an even deeper instinct; he was in inner danger—the fall from the heights of pride to the depths of humiliation."6 Columbus's tact was rewarded, for even though Fray Buil had accused him of withholding food from anyone who contradicted him, and even though the king and queen were angered by the five hundred slaves on Torres's ships, Columbus was well received. As a result of his excellent relationship with the king and queen, particularly the queen, he was able to convince them to finance a third expedition.

This third expedition, which finally got underway on May 30, 1498, proved to be the most trying and the most humiliating for Columbus and his two brothers. During this period they came into serious conflict with other men whom Ferdinand and Isabella sent over to help govern. Bartholomew, in Hispaniola, continued to fight the native uprisings by impressing captives as slaves. Francisco Roldan, with seventy rebels, established his own town, Xaragua, in direct opposition to Columbus's orders, posing a serious threat to

Columbus's authority. But perhaps the most distressing matter for Columbus and his brothers was that the rebels referred to them as Conversos. Columbus counterattacked, calling Roldan and his men Conversos. Madariaga suggests that Columbus's difficulty in governing was tied to the Spaniards' identification of Columbus and his brothers as Conversos. Madariaga writes:

> As was to be expected, the people in revolt against the Colóns soon discovered their Jewish origin. We know that anti-semitism was always a democratic, and pro-semitism an aristocratic attitude in Spain. It was therefore to be expected that in Española the "gentlemen and men of quality" would be with Colón and the people against him. We know that the Admiral was attacked as a *Converso* because he says so himself in a sentence the very obscurity of which is most suggestive; for Colón starts defending himself against the accusation before he has let out that he had been accused; and he at once counter-attacks: "But this would not be so if the author of the discovery had been a *Converso*, because *Conversos* are enemies of Your Highnesses and of Christians, but they spread that name and in such a way that all was lost; and these men who are with Roldán, who is now raising trouble against me, they say most of them are [*Conversos*]." He is on the defensive. . . . But despite his denials, there are signs . . . that the Spanish colony in Española remained convinced, that the Colons were of Jewish extraction.[7]

It is thus possible that Columbus and his brothers had trouble commanding the Spaniards because they were identified as Conversos and were therefore not respected. When

Columbus tried to rally an army to fight against Francisco Roldan, the men would not follow him. His authority was so limited that all he could do was extract a promise from Roldan to return to Spain with his rebellious men and slaves. Columbus had planned to send a secret letter to the king and queen, recommending that upon his arrival, Roldan be arrested for his revolt. Roldan, however, never sailed for Spain but ended up demanding to be made Alcalde Mayor of Hispaniola, to which Columbus ultimately capitulated. The humiliating compromise with Roldan further weakened his already tenuous position as governor. Certainly if Columbus was from a Converso family, it would have been difficult for him to rule, as indeed it was. He finally decided it was imperative for him to present his case to the king and queen. He was preparing to sail back to Spain when Isabela faced an uprising from the native people. At about this same time, Alonso de Hojedo returned to Hispaniola, and, sensing Columbus's vulnerable state, threatened another revolt.

In response to the growing unrest, Christopher and Bartholomew ordered brutal punishments and death sentences. Adrian de Muxica, a young nobleman who was part of the rebellion, was executed by being thrown from a tower. Columbus violently kicked Ximeno, an officer of Don Juan de Fonseca (court official in charge of Indian affairs). Some men were starved, others were hanged, and native people were tortured and enslaved.

All of these incidents were reported back to Ferdinand and Isabella, rulers who were well acquainted with iron fisted policies. They had been merciless at times, in order to accomplish their goals. The Jewish expulsion, the constant autos de fé, the brutal police force of the Hermandad had already stained the hands of Ferdinand and Isabella. But their concern over the ability of Columbus and his brothers to rule effectively continued to grow. Queen Isabella was distressed also over Columbus's disregard of her order to stop the slave trade. The monarchs now decided to send Francisco de Bobadilla to Hispaniola to assess the deteriorating situation. Before Bobadilla set sail, further reports made it increasingly clear that Columbus had lost control over the colony. They gave Bobadilla permission to take over the role of governor if he deemed it necessary. Bobadilla was given permission to order Columbus to "surrender all forts, houses, ships, arms, munitions, supplies, horses, cattle and other things belonging to Their Highnesses."[8] The monarchs clearly intended to have Bobadilla take Columbus's place as governor.

* * *

When Bobadilla landed and summoned Columbus, Christopher wrote a letter to his brother, Bartholomew, in unknown characters, discussing the delicate situation. There has been much controversy as to the language of these unknown characters. Columbus's contemporary, Peter Martyr, recorded, ". . . the new Governor has sent the King and Queen letters written by the Admiral in unknown characters, in which he warned and advised his brother the Adelantado, who was away, to come with armed forces to defend him against any affront in case the Governor intended to attack him by violence."[9] Madariaga suggests that the characters were Hebrew cursive script. He notes:

It is well known that in some Spanish-Jewish colonies newspapers are published in Spanish, though written in

Jewish script, which justifies the assumption that the
Colón family might have kept some knowledge of Hebrew script while knowing no Hebrew. . . . Evidently a
normal Jewish script would have been dangerous for
Colón and his brother to use; but a more or less illegible
cursive hand in Hebrew characters would have been
quite safe.[10]

Could the letter have been written in Hebrew? There are
other indications that Columbus may have had some knowledge of Hebrew, which will be further examined. But for
now, whatever language this letter was written in, Columbus
clearly felt threatened and was preparing to defend himself
against the Crown, which was represented by Bobadilla.
Columbus disputed Bobadilla's claim as the new governor,
but Bobadilla was not going to argue. Instead, he arrested
both Christopher and Diego. Shortly thereafter, when Bartholomew arrived in Isabela, he, too, was arrested. In October of the year 1500, Columbus and his two brothers, fet-
tered in irons, were placed on board the caravel *La Gorda*
and thus disgraced, were transported to Spain.

13

STUDENT OF THE OLD TESTAMENT

1451–1506

Columbus's signature: Note the triangular shape. Dots placed beside each S are thought to be part of a disguised blessing.

Bound in chains, Columbus turned to the Old Testament for comfort. In a 1501 letter he wrote, "And Jeremiah says again: At that time they shall call Jerusalem the throne of the Lord: and all the nations shall be gathered unto it, to the name of the Lord, to Jerusalem; neither shall they walk any more after the imagination of their evil heart."[1] At this moment of greatest humiliation, he focused on his desire to set Jerusalem free. It seems almost a messianic desire and certainly it is a particularly Jewish passion to return to Jerusalem. In the same letter, he referred to Isaiah, including the passage: "And in that day there shall be a root of Jesse which shall stand for an ensign of the people: to it shall the Gentiles seek; and his rest shall be glorious. And it shall come to pass in that day that the

187

Lord shall set His hand again the second time to recover the remnant of His people which shall be left, from Assyria, and from Egypt [. . .] and from the islands of the sea."[2] The messianic reference is clear, and Columbus seems to have felt that he was an important instrument of God in helping to bring His people back to Jerusalem. In his numerous audiences with the king and queen, Columbus evoked the city of Jerusalem as the main quest both he and the Catholic Monarchs sought. These references to the Old Testament, to the prophets rather than to the New Testament, make one question his background once again.

Throughout most of Columbus's life he made numerous references to the Old Testament. Even in his younger days in Portugal, Columbus made three separate entries in the margins of d'Ailly's *Imago Mundi* that were Jewish in nature. Columbus wrote, "Jericho, a town which has become famous owing to Jeremiah. . . ." Further down on the page he wrote, "many Jewish places mentioned," and again, "All peoples received their astronomy from the Jews." He also made reference to the small size of the Jews' Promised Land.[3] He focused not only on the Jewish references in d'Ailly's work but, even more importantly, he actually used the prophets to help put together his scheme to sail west.

After he had arrived back in Spain, in 1502, he wrote to Ferdinand and Isabella that "in carrying out of this enterprise of the Indies neither reason nor mathematics nor maps were any use to me: fully accomplished were the words of Isaiah."[4] Certainly Columbus was influenced by the prophets Isaiah and Jeremiah from the Old Testament.

Even though the Jews had rejected the apocryphal book of *Esdras*, Columbus studied it carefully and took its words quite literally. He expected the world to be only one-seventh under water. His faith in the book's words was so strong that he calculated the amount of dry land versus water as described in *Esdras* and expected to find land between 600 and 700 leagues from the Canary Islands on his first voyage.[5] From the time Columbus presented his work to King Joao II and then eventually to Ferdinand and Isabella, he claimed to have a secret that had eluded other explorers. Some scholars suggest that Columbus was referring to Esdras's estimation of the ocean. Columbus even felt that Toscanelli, though on the right track, had not properly figured out the distance because he had not considered *Esdras*. As Madariaga notes, "Colon, through his study of Esdras [Ezra], knew that the distance was only 2550 miles."[6] Columbus was clearly basing his calculations on the prophetic words of *Esdras*.

Continuous Jewish references to the Old Testament were made throughout his lifetime of writing. As previously mentioned in his first, most famous letter to Ferdinand and Isabella he wrote, "And thus, having expelled all the Jews from all your kingdoms and dominions, in the same month of January Your Highnesses commanded me that with a sufficient fleet I should go to the said parts of India. . . ."[7] When the Jews were expelled from Spain, the Church and the Inquisition became omnipotent. Because he referred to the Jews and the expulsion without specific approval or adulation for the action taken by the crown, the suggestion arises that Columbus may have identified with the exiled Jews. Adulation would have been expected within the Royal Court. His words were tactless. It is almost as if he was insinuating that he, too, was leaving Spain just as the Jews were being forced to leave. Once again, his words suggest that he might have been of Jewish extraction. Referring to this opening of his letter and his lack of adulation, Madariaga writes, "this silence is as good as a confession, and in those days it was dangerous enough."[8] The Spanish Inquisition had, by this time, infiltrated every aspect of life, and Columbus was indeed taking a grave risk in referring to the expulsion so boldly with no flattery for the king and queen or, at the very least, a condemnation of the Jews who were expelled.

Columbus continued to lean heavily on the writings of the Old Testament. When he had been out to sea for just a short while on his first voyage, the men began to worry that the fair winds blowing them westward would never carry them back. Fear and anxiety must have gripped the common sailor in 1492. The elite, the well-educated men in the 1490s, accepted the idea that the earth was round and that theoretically, it was possible to sail westward to reach the Indies. But Columbus was not just trying to sail three wooden caravels across the Atlantic Ocean. He had to combat not only the waves and uncharted winds but also the superstitions and fears that gripped the men on board all three ships. The constant westerly winds frightened the sailors but when the winds changed direction, the sailors' fears were assuaged. Columbus was so relieved to have had some convincing natural phenomena take place that he wrote in his diary, "So this high sea was very necessary to me, for this had not happened except at the time of the Jews, when they went out of Egypt with Moses who was leading them out of captivity."[9] The high sea had saved Columbus from an early mutiny, and he knew it. This passage provides significant insight into some of his innermost thoughts. Columbus identified with Moses. It was the Old Testament that gave him strength during this stressful stage of the voyage.

In his prayers on that first voyage he turned to Psalm 107: "They that go down to the sea in ships and occupy their business in great water; these men see the works of the Lord, and his wonder in the deep."[10] It was a psalm that comforted him.

There are discrepancies between the private Columbus and the public man. After land was first sighted, and they laid anchor, Columbus placed a cross at the entrance to the harbor. He wrote to the king and queen that they would "propagate the holy Christian religion . . . (by) converting such great peoples."[11] This is certainly the side Columbus wanted the world to see, to know, and to recognize. In his formal plans for colonizing the New World, he wrote, "And I say that Your Highnesses ought not to consent that any foreigner do business or set foot here, except Christian Catholics, since this was the end and the beginning of the enterprise, that it should be for the enhancement and glory of the Christian religion, nor should anyone who is not a good Christian come to these parts."[12] Was this statement meant for the eyes of the Inquisition, meant to reassure and appease Isabella? Could Columbus have had an ulterior motive for wanting to discover new land, a land where the Jews would be safe from the Inquisition? Many Conversos and Jews did make their way to the New World. Sadly, the Inquisition doggedly followed them. As previously stated, Columbus was born and raised a Catholic. If he was from a Converso family, he was also a believer in Christ. But still, a Jewish orientation toward his reading and writing persisted.

On his third ill-fated voyage to the New World, he was beginning to realize that he had, in fact, discovered a vast land. Again he turned to *Esdras* to find some explanation for what he had found. He wrote, "I am convinced that this is mainland, very large, unknown heretofore, and reason helps me greatly on account of this great river and sea, which is fresh, and then I draw help also from the saying of Esdras in Book IV, Chapter 6, which says that six parts of the earth are dry and one under water, a book approved of by St. Ambrose and St. Augustine."[13] The two saints are referred to almost as an afterthought, as if he knew the Inquisition would have access to the letters addressed to the king and queen.

Columbus had always been obsessed with liberating Jerusalem from the infidels. In his first audience with Ferdinand and Isabella his greatest argument for sponsoring the enterprise was that he would discover gems and gold which would, in turn, finance a crusade for the liberation of Jerusalem. On his first voyage, the *Santa Maria* was shipwrecked, but in his anguish over losing the ship, he wrote a letter to the king and queen, reiterating his grand passion. He wrote, "I declared to Your Highnesses that all the gain of this my Enterprise should be spent in the conquest of Jerusalem."[14] This passion to capture Jerusalem persisted throughout his life.

Marooned in Jamaica on his fourth voyage, he wrote yet another letter to the king and queen in which he said, "Who was ever born, not excepting Job, who did not die in despair."[15] This voyage had been the most harrowing because of the wild tropical storms and hostile native people. Columbus had turned his caravels into fortresses and had sent for help. He had developed a high fever and the native people would not supply the ship with food. In the following letter, dated July 7, 1503, one can feel his desperation. In this weakened state, he claimed to have heard a voice that said:

Oh fool, man slow to believe and to serve thy God, God of all! What more did He do for Moses or for David His servant? From thy birth, He always took great care of thee. When He saw thee of an age which satisfied Him, marvellously did He make thy name resound in the Earth. The Indies, which are part of the world, so rich, He gave them to thee as thine; thou gavest them to whomsoever thou didst please and He gave thee power to do so. Of the shackles of the Ocean Sea, which were bound with such strong chains, He gave thee the keys; and thou wast obeyed in so many lands and didst win such honoured renown amongst Christians! What more did He do for the people of Israel when He led them out of Egypt? Nor for David, whom from a shepherd He raised to be King of Judea? Turn thy face to Him and know thy error at last: His mercy is boundless: thy age shall not hinder great things: He has many very great mansions. Abraham was over a hundred when he begat Isaac, and Sarah, was she a girl? Thou callest out for uncertain help: answer, who has afflicted thee so much and so often, God or the World? The privileges and promises which God gives, He breaks them not, nor does He say, after He has received the service, that His intention was different and that it must be understood in another way, nor does He give martyrdom to anyone in order to lend some colour to sheer force: He sticks to the letter; all He promises, He fulfills and more: is this customary? I have said what thy Creator has done for thee and does for all. Now He will show some of the reward of this anxiety and danger which thou hast undergone serving others.[16]

This voice is very much a Judaic voice. All the references to the Old Testament, to Moses, David, Abraham, Isaac, and Sarah are Judaic. Not once does the voice mention Christ.

Instead, the voice speaks of the "God of all," not of a Holy Trinity. The voice speaks of winning honor among Christians (as if they were separate from him) and asks, "What more did He do for the people of Israel when He led them out of Egypt?" It seems that in the height of his fever, all Columbus could hear was a sorrowful voice longing for peace with the "God of all." It is remarkable that Columbus wrote this down, for the Inquisition could have had access to it.

As he aged, his references consistently remained tied to the Old Testament and not to the New. He referred to the book of Kings, to Solomon, and again to David. He wrote, "David in his testament left three thousand hundred-weights of gold of the Indies to Solomon, as a contribution to the building of the temple, and according to Josephus, it was the gold of these lands. Jerusalem and Mount Sion are to be rebuilt by Christian hands: whose hands, God by the mouth of the Prophet says in the fourteenth Psalm."[17] Again, the Jerusalem passion surfaces.

Even the staunchest critics of his Judaic background take some note. Though Morison derides those who question Columbus's Jewish extraction, he remarks that after the third voyage Columbus likened himself to David because he was never able to please his king. Morison writes, "Columbus sometimes compared himself to David, who was commanded to perform incredible tasks for Saul, and performed them; yet at each success fell deeper and deeper into disfavor."[18] Columbus did not envision himself as a Christian martyr but rather like King David.

Columbus grasped the significance of his discoveries better than any of his contemporaries. He had seen with his own eyes the vast potential of the New World. But he was not politically savvy, and had made enemies every step of the way. As he became older and frailer, his defenses were lowered and his writings seem to reflect his true feelings.

* * *

It would seem that if Columbus were of Jewish extraction, or even a Marrano, he would have slipped somewhere in his writings. Indeed there does seem to be such a slip. In his copy of Pope Pius II's *Historia Rerum*, Columbus reckoned the age of the world as 5241, which was the Jewish calendar reckoning. Columbus wrote, "and from the destruction of the Second House according to the Jews to the present day, being the year of the birth of Our Lord 1481, are 1413 years."[19] Cecil Roth notes that the Jews referred to the Second House, whereas Christians referred to "the Destruction of Jerusalem."[20] Roth further notes that the Christians had the more accurate dating of the destruction of the Second Temple at the year 70 and that the Jewish dating of the destruction of the Temple was the year 68.[21] Columbus was clearly using the Jewish rather than the Christian system of reckoning the destruction of the Second Temple. Also, Columbus figured this reckoning in 1481 before he traveled to Spain. As Roth concludes, "It is not easy to explain this except on the assumption that his was a semi-Jewish family."[22] In other words, it seems that Columbus must have had some Jewish background in order to have come up with this system of dating.

This does not mean that Columbus was in fact a secret Jew but strongly suggests that he was of Jewish extraction. His constant Judaic references, his passion to liberate Jerusalem and his system of reckoning the destruction of the Second Temple all lend credence to the argument that he was of Spanish-Jewish descent.

14

COLUMBUS'S FOURTH VOYAGE AND FINAL YEARS

1500–1506

Letter to Columbus's son Diego and detail. This notation at the top of his personal letters looks remarkably like the old Hebrew script *Bet Heh*. Marranos were known to place the blessing of a *Bet Heh* at the top of letters to loved ones.

Feeling the weight of iron chains about him, Columbus somberly disembarked the caravel, *La Gorda*, in Cadiz, in the fall of 1500. He remained bound in chains until December 12, when Ferdinand and Isabella discovered that he was still incarcerated and ordered his release. The monarchs sent 2,000 ducats so that he might come to them in Granada.[1] The humble robes of a Franciscan monk would seem offensive for a man who had been bound in chains, and so he dressed in discreet attire and arrived in Granada on December 17 in time for an audience with the monarchs. As he walked into the throne room to be received, it seems he was so overwhelmed with grief that he bowed on his knees before them. In a gentle voice, Ferdinand bade him to rise. When he heard a kind word from the king, he broke down before the monarchs and wept. The monarchs expressed great sympathy for all Columbus had suffered, but would not reinstate him as governor. It was clear to everyone at Court that Columbus was a valuable admiral but an incompetent administrator.

To Columbus's chagrin, the monarchs appointed Don Nicolas de Ovando to take his place. This was a crushing blow for Columbus but the monarchs were still prepared to sponsor one more voyage of discovery. More than a year after his return, on March 14, 1502, the monarchs commanded that he set out once again, this time concentrating on finding a strait to the Pacific Ocean. They insisted that he not go near Hispaniola until he had to resupply his ships for the voyage home. Ferdinand and Isabella hoped Columbus would find a passage through the Indies and sail around the world.

Commanding four caravels, Columbus left Seville on April 3, 1502. His thirteen-year-old son, Ferdinand, accompanied him on this voyage, while his other son, Diego, stayed home to represent him at Court.

It was ironic that Columbus reached Hispaniola at the end of June, just as an armada was preparing to leave with Columbus's rival, the ex-governor Bobadilla. Bobadilla's flagship carried a cargo of 200,000 castellanos in gold.[2] Columbus warned the armada not to set sail, for he saw an approaching storm and asked, at the same time, for a safe harbor. Governor Ovando denied Columbus a safe harbor, upholding the king and queen's command that he not land until his return voyage. Ovando also ignored Columbus's warning of dangerous seas and sent the armada off to Spain. Certainly those who scoffed at Columbus when he gave warning sorely regretted not having listened to the seasoned admiral, for the armada carrying Bobadilla was lost in the raging storm. The only ship that survived carried gold marked for Columbus and was eventually delivered to his son, Diego. It was the only gold delivered from what had been the gallant armada, carrying the largest amount of gold up to that time. Columbus also must have been grief-stricken when he heard of the disaster, for his trusted friend, Antonio de Torres, had been the captain of the flagship that had carried Bobadilla.

It is fascinating to see how Columbus did survive the storm. Forbidden to land in Hispaniola, he turned his ships round to the leeward side of the island. Though his ships were buffeted, the island protected them from destruction. After a few days of rest, he began his quest to find Cathay and the mythological strait to the Pacific Ocean. He sailed past Jamaica and then on to the islands off Honduras. In these waters he encountered more than a month of raging storms. Keeping his journal as best he could, he wrote at this time:

> The ships lay exposed to the weather, with sails torn, and anchors, rigging, cables, boats and many of the stores lost; the people exhausted and so down in the mouth that they were all the time making vows to be good, to go on pilgrimages and all that; yea, even hearing one another's confessions! Other tempests I have seen, but none that lasted so long or so grim as this. Many old hands whom we looked on as stout fellows lost their courage. What gripped me most were the sufferings of my son; to think that so young a lad, only thirteen, should go through so much. But Our Lord lent him such courage that he even heartened the rest, and he worked as though he had been to sea all of a long life.

> That comforted me. I was sick and many times lay at
> death's door, but gave orders from a dog house that the
> people clapped together for me on the poop deck. My
> brother was in the worst of the ships, the cranky one,
> and I felt terribly having persuaded him to come against
> his will.[3]

Undaunted by the stormy weather, Columbus continued to
search for a strait to the Pacific Ocean. Finally the weather
grew fair and Columbus took full advantage of the calm sea.
He sailed down the coast of Nicaragua, past Costa Rica to
what is now the mouth of the Panama Canal. Another of the
great ironies in Columbus's life was that here the native
people convinced him that no such strait to the Pacific
Ocean existed, and he ceased to look for a passageway.
Only thirteen years later, in 1513, Vasco Nunez de Balboa
returned to Panama and set out across the land to discover
the Pacific Ocean. But at this moment in 1502, Columbus
turned his attention to the search for gold.

Columbus now sailed his fleet up the Belen River which
runs between Panama and Costa Rica. He laid anchor and
sent Bartholomew upriver to look for gold. Fulfilling Columbus's expectations, Bartholomew found the gold mines of
the Guaymis people. Columbus decided to settle a town at
the place where he had laid anchor and called it Santa Maria
de Belen. Here the native population did not perceive the
Spaniards as men from heaven and were angered by the idea
of a settlement. To complicate the situation, one of the
vessels, the *Gallega*, ran upon a sand bar so that Columbus
could not escape without abandoning the grounded ship. A
scouting party, which was sent ashore to fetch fresh food
and water, was attacked. Suffering from malaria, Columbus

waited in vain for the party to return, and in a state of delirium, he wrote the passage with references to Moses and David, quoted in greater length in the preceding chapter. He wrote about a voice that cried out to him, questioning what more did God do for Moses, David, and the people of Israel. As noted earlier, in desperate circumstances Columbus's references seem to have Judaic overtones. The references to every man as opposed to Christian men, to Moses, to the people of Israel, and to David King of Israel all suggest a deeply rooted Judaic orientation.

When only one man returned from the scouting party to report on the massacre, Columbus abandoned hope of rescuing the *Gallega*. He recalled his brother Bartholomew, who had been desperately trying to secure the town, Santa Maria de Belen. With the loss of ten men, Columbus sailed away from Belen and headed for Hispaniola. But the ships were worm-eaten and leaking, his men hungry for fresh food and water, so Columbus was forced to lay anchor in Jamaica. The ships were beached in the place he named Puerto Santa Gloria, and he allowed his men to trek inland in search of fresh water and game. With little more than a prayer, Columbus sent Diego Mendez in a large canoe to try and reach Hispaniola. Miraculously, after a hundred mile trip, Mendez made it, but Governor Ovando delayed a rescue ship for nine months.

During these months of waiting and wondering if Mendez even reached Hispaniola, Columbus turned the beached ships into a protruding fortification. The bulky wooden caravels were all the Spaniards had to protect themselves from a hostile native population. A few months after Mendez had paddled away, fifty men formed a conspiracy, accused Columbus of keeping them on the island against their will and, like Mendez, departed in canoes with hopes of making it to Hispaniola. The mutineers, however, had the poor judgment of setting out in January. Shortly after they had taken off, they were wrecked upon the seas and only a few men staggered back to Columbus in Santa Gloria.

The most serious problem Columbus faced while waiting for a rescue party, however, was the lack of fresh food and water. In February the native people decided they would no longer supply the little fort but Columbus quickly devised a ruse to keep supplies coming in. With his copy of *Ephemerides*, a book predicting eclipses, by Abraham Zacuto, he noted an eclipse was due to occur on February 29. He called the native people together and threatened to take away the moon if they did not supply the Spaniards with food and water. The eclipse occurred as predicted and the terrified people supplied the Spaniards until they were rescued. On June 29 Mendez was allowed finally to send a caravel to Jamaica. Columbus and his men returned to Hispaniola and then charted another ship to take them home to Spain. They departed on September 12, 1504, arriving in Spain on November 7, just nineteen days before Queen Isabella died. Isabella had been Columbus's greatest ally, his most ardent supporter. With her death he knew his chances for another voyage were gone.

Columbus now began to concentrate on petitioning the king to honor the original Capitulations of Santa Fe, but his poor health interfered with his ability to travel with the Royal Court. The stress and strain of the fourth voyage had taken a great toll on his health.

During the last two years of his life, he made a significant effort to put his affairs in order and curious symbols began to appear in his writing. For example, he began to sign his name in a triangular fashion, demanding that his heirs use this signature in perpetuity. The signature is as follows:

.S.

S.A.S.

X M Y

Xp̃o FERENS[4]

At the time, it was customary to sign legal documents, "In the name of the Holy Trinity." Some scholars believe this ending is represented in the first initials. The Latin interpretation, "Servus Supplex Altissimi Salvatoris,"[5] translates to "Humble Servant of the Most High Savior." The "Xp̃o FERENS," they believe, was meant to represent Columbus as the Christ-bearer.[6] But Madariaga and the noted scholar Maurice David offer different interpretations. Madariaga investigated the matter by going back to the original instructions Columbus gave his son, Diego, in which Columbus wrote:

> Don Diego, my son, or anyone who may inherit this entail, after having inherited and obtained possession of it, shall sign my signature which I now use, which is an X, with an S above, and an M, with a Roman A above, and above it an S, and then a Greek Y, with an S above it, with their strokes and commas as I do now and as will be seen by my signatures and by the one hereafter. And he will write nothing but *The Admiral*, even though the King might give him, or he might win, other titles.[7]

Madariaga notes that the S's were always between dots and that S's also appeared in some of Columbus's marginal notes concerning Judea and Majorca. He writes, "There is not the slightest doubt that the letter S had a special significance for him."[8] David concurs and adds that the Jewish Star of David is often used with the letter S. His explanation helps to substantiate Madariaga's suggestion that the S in Columbus's signature had special significance. David writes:

> This very S . . . leads to the solution of the strange and mystic signature, which means nothing else but the last confession of the Jews as read from right to left with Hebrew words for each initial—abbreviated, it is true— but perfectly acceptable, according to the rabbinical laws. . . . it is meant simultaneously as a Kaddish for Colon—or better, as a substitute for a Kaddish—the supreme prayer dreamed of continually by all Jews alike. . . . Hence the repeated command to his heirs and their heirs to sign exactly like his signature always and perpetually.[9]

David suggests that because the Inquisition investigated every aspect of a person's private life, Columbus's sons would never be able to say Kaddish, the mourner's prayer, for him. David indicates that the signature was a substitute for a Kaddish. His theory is based on the fact that Marranos were known to use signatures for just such a purpose. David suggests that the signature actually stood for the Hebrew supplication in praise of God:

Shadai, Shadai
Adonoy Shadai
Yehova molai chesed
Nauthai ovon, pesha, chatuo[10]

Shadai, Adonoy and *Yehova* are all Jewish names for God. *Molai chesed* can be translated as full of compassion. *Nauthai ovon, pesha, chatuo* can be translated as forgive iniquity, crime, and sin. This triangular signature might have represented a blessing Columbus intended to pass down to his sons to be used in perpetuity. David writes, "Rabbinical laws, preoccupied especially with religious oppression, and the mental sufferings of the hundreds of thousands [of] enforced conversos, expressly allowed such abbreviation of the 'last confession.'"[11] While this prayer is not the mourner's kaddish, it is possible that Columbus was asking his sons to perpetuate the signature in praise of God as a substitute for the mourner's kaddish. Columbus may have been privy to subterfuges invented for Jewish blessings that he intended to pass onto his sons.

Madariaga and David also note the triangular shape of the signature. They suggest the triangle might represent the triangular Shield of the Star of David. David writes, "The shape of the signature as prescribed by Colon forms a perfect triangle-figure sacred to the Jews and used by them on the front of synagogues, on church vessels for sacramental wine, and on gravestones."[12] Concerning the triangular shape of Columbus's signature, Madariaga states, "The first thing that strikes the eye in this signature is its triangular character. It inevitably leads the mind to the Cabbala. Thus does Colón himself, by strict adherence to a most unusual practice, lead the least prepossessed observer to the chief occult science of the Jews."[13]

David also explored the "Xр̄o FERENS" part of the signature. He suggests that if Columbus meant the signature to mean Christ-bearer, as other scholars have speculated, then Columbus would have included the customary cross on his coat of arms. But Columbus did not have the cross on his coat of arms. David suggests rather that Columbus was secretly referring to the last line of the Hebrew phrase, "*nauthey ovon, pesha, chatuo.*"[14] Roth does not give much credit to this line of thinking because David's interpretation of the letters is a supplication and not a kaddish. Roth suggests that the S.S.A.S. might have stood for "Sanctus, Sanctus, Sanctus Adonai—'Holy, Holy, Holy is the Lord,' [i.e., 'of Hosts']. . . . the X in the next line would presumably stand for *Christus*, in its very common Greek form *Xristos*, and the M for *Maria*. . . . the line would stand for . . . 'Christ, son of Mary.'"[15] While Roth vacillates on the meaning of the signature, he does agree with David and Madariaga that the signature and other notations Columbus made were used by the Marranos. This suggests that Columbus may have had some knowledge of Jewish mysticism. One must not forget that even personal letters in the fifteenth and sixteenth centuries could have fallen into the hands of the Inquisition, so subterfuges for Jewish prayers were commonly used.

Besides the signature, a curious mark in the upper left-hand corner of Columbus's letters to his son Diego may also have been a Jewish form of prayer. David suggests that the symbol is a Hebrew *Bet Heh*. Roth notes that the *Bet Heh* represents the blessing, "*beEzrath haShem* . . . With the help of God."[16] This symbol only appears on letters to Diego and is missing on Diego's one letter that was intended also for the eyes of the king and queen. Both scholars note that it was a common Jewish practice to place a *Bet Heh* in the upper left-hand corner of a letter to a loved one. David suggests that this notation is further evidence of Columbus's Jewish origins. While Roth believes the notation may have been nothing more than a library marking, he does note that this custom was practiced by the Marranos.

Several points fixed in his will also suggest that Columbus may have been of Jewish extraction. He asked that one-tenth of his income be distributed to the poor. David points out that giving one-tenth of one's income or "tithing" has deep roots in Jewish tradition. David writes, "Tithing one's possessions is a very ancient custom, existing as early as the time of the patriarch Abraham, and Jacob made a vow that, if he should return to his father's house in safety, he would acknowledge Jehova as his Lord and would give Him a tenth of everything he possessed."[17] Columbus also wanted to provide a dowry for poor girls and specifically asked that, "it must be given to them in such a way that they do not notice wherefrom it comes."[18] Providing poor girls with a dowry is also an old Jewish custom, as David notes, "the provision for a 'dowry' or 'nedunya' for poor girls to facilitate their marriage, is also foreseen in the rabbinical laws."[19] But perhaps the most suggestive clause in the will is Columbus's desire to leave money to "a Jew who lived at the entrance of the Ghetto in Lisbon, the equivalent of one half mark in silver."[20] Though the amount is not great, it seems that Columbus passed many times in and out of the Jewish ghetto in Lisbon, enough times to come to know the Jew at the entrance, and he wished to remember him. Once again, we wonder if he went in and out of the ghetto on business, perhaps to see Don Isaac Abravanel or other influential men? Could he have had a more secret reason for visiting the ghetto, such as attending a religious service? We don't know why he visited the ghetto so often but whatever the reasons were, Columbus wished to remember the Jew at Lisbon's ghetto gate.

King Ferdinand kept the matter of Columbus's rights to the wealth from the dominions he discovered tied up in the courts. When Queen Isabella's daughter, the Infanta Juana, held Court in Valladolid, Columbus followed her there, hoping to convince her to reinstate the rights granted to him in the Capitulations. But since he had fallen ill, Bartholomew went in his place. On May 19, Columbus reviewed his will, giving last instructions to his sons, making sure he had provided for his beloved Beatriz Enriquez de Harana and others he wanted to remember. On the following day, May 20, 1506, Columbus received the last rites and died shortly thereafter.

15

COLUMBUS'S LEGACY—THE SEPHARDIM IN THE NEW WORLD

1502–1654

Dutch merchant ship of the seventeenth century, carrying Jews to New Amsterdam in 1654.

In 1502 Juan Sanchez of Saragossa bowed before King Ferdinand and gratefully received permission to establish trading posts in the New World. With five caravels carrying wheat, barley, and horses, Juan set out to establish trade with the native people. He was a secret Jew.[1] Juan's uncle was Gabriel Sanchez, the Converso who was King Ferdinand's treasurer. Juan's father was implicated in the murder of Fray Pedro Arbues, Canon of the Cathedral of Saragossa, and had died in an auto de fé in Saragossa.

After Juan Sanchez established active trade with the native population, other Conversos who were noblemen, physicians, merchants, and farmers were quick to follow. Another early secret Jewish settler was Columbus's translator, Luis de Torres, who received a large tract of land in

Cuba where he lived until his death.[2] While Columbus's initial intention may or may not have been to find a safe haven for Jews, the Sephardim did come to the New World in hopes of escaping the Inquisition. Indeed, it seemed even the Crown was prepared to accept the flight of the Conversos, for in 1509 an agreement was reached between King Ferdinand and the Conversos whereby they were allowed to emigrate for a two-year period if they paid the Crown 20,000 ducats.[3] After crossing the ocean, the Conversos quickly returned to practicing their Judaism.

When the word spread that Judaism was flourishing in the New World, Marranos fled Spain and Portugal, settling in some of the earliest outposts in Cuba, Jamaica, Barbados, Tobago, Martinique, Curacao, Mexico, Brazil, Surinam, and Peru. But as these thinly disguised Jewish communities grew, the Spanish and Portuguese Royal Crowns were determined to stop them. Queen Isabella's two daughters, Queen Isabella in Portugal and Queen Juana (married to Philip of Hapsburg), encouraged the Inquisition to move aggressively against the Marranos. When Queen Isabella in Portugal insisted that all Jews be baptized, she unleashed such unprecedented terror that many Marranos sacrificed everything in order to escape to the New World. And in 1511, Queen Juana in Spain ordered the Inquisition to be established in Hispaniola. Kayserling notes, "Queen Juana of Spain was obliged to adopt measures against the secret Jews, 'the sons and grandsons of the burned,' who held public offices. Every secret Jew who, without the permission of the crown, was in possession of such an office, was to lose it, and was, furthermore, to be punished with the confiscation of his property."[4] Confiscation of property was only the prelude to their punishment, for then they were turned over to the Inquisition.

By 1515, the Inquisition was arresting Marranos in Hispaniola. Once arrested, they were sent back to Spain to face a tribunal. By 1518 the Hispaniola Inquisition was prepared to try cases and carry out autos de fé. Hernando Alonso, a conquistador who accompanied Cortes to Mexico, was one of the first Judaizers to be burned at the stake in the New World.[5] From the very earliest days of Spanish and Portuguese rule, the Inquisition became just as powerful in the New World as it continued to be in the Old.

By 1567 it had become obvious to the Portuguese Crown that the flight of the Conversos would not be stopped solely by the Inquisition. On June 30, 1567, the Crown declared that no Converso could leave for the New World without leaving behind heavy collateral. As Kayserling notes:

> Not until the Jews and Marranos in the colonies offered to pay the state the enormous sum of 1,700,000 cruzados, was the prohibition to migrate rescinded by the law of May 21, 1577. This law allowed them freedom of residence and of trade; in the future, no one was to call them Jews, New Christians, or Marranos.[6]

King Philip II, a grandson of Queen Juana, hoped that the combined effort of this new order, plus an aggressive Inquisition, would finally put an end to Judaizing in the New World. During the 1580s, autos de fé were carried out in earnest. Some specific family names found were Juan Alvarez of Zafra, along with his wife, children, and nephew, who were burned at the stake in Lima, Peru, Manuel Lopez of Yelves, Portugal, as well as Duarte Nunez de Cea, Alvaro Nunez of Braganza, Diego Nunez de Silva and Diego Rodriguez de Silveyra, who all confessed that they practiced Judaism and died as martyrs.[7] Of the Marrano Nunez de Cea, Kayserling records that, "before ascending the funeral pyre he confessed that as a Jew he had lived, observing the precepts of Judaism, and that it was his simple wish to die a Jew, as his ancestors had done."[8] We can only imagine the horror felt at seeing loved ones ascending a pyre, being tied to the stake, facing a torturous death by fire. But these men, women, and children faced death with courage and remained steadfast to the very end. They were true martyrs. The mournful words of the martyr Gabriel de Granada offer a haunting remembrance.

> Lord, my soul called upon Thee to deliver me from the fire and flame that I may not be burned or scorched. Here I am in this desert turned into a plant where great trouble shall overtake me. They shall cast me into thick darkness where neither brother nor cousin can aught avail me. I ask of Thee, my God, one thing—that Thou remember my soul.[9]

Perhaps the most celebrated case of martyrdom in the New World was that of Luis de Carvajal, nephew and namesake of the governor of the Province of Nuevo Leon, Mexico. The governor, Luis de Carvajal, was one of the first conquistadors to explore and settle a massive area of Mexico. In his work *The Martyr*, the noted scholar Dr. Martin Cohen writes, "The territory embraced all of the contemporary Mexican states of Nuevo Leon and Tamaulipas, almost all of Coahuila . . . part of San Luis Potosi. . . . and Spain's Florida Territory."[10] Carvajal's vast territory even included sections of today's Texas and New Mexico. On March 13, 1589, the governor's niece, Isabel, was charged with heresy and arrested by the Inquisition. It seems that most of the Carvajal family were secret Jews. Concerning the young Luis de Carvajal, Cohen writes:

> Nearly everyone else in his family, though officially and publicly Catholic, were secret Jews—his parents, his sisters, his brother Baltasar, and numerous cousins who had emigrated with them from Spain in the summer of 1580. And so was he. Even his uncle, arrested earlier in the year for political reasons, had been quietly whisked away to the inquisitional prison, an almost certain sign that he too was suspected of having betrayed his catholic faith."[11]

The governor denied taking part in any Jewish practices, but he was well aware of his family's Judaizing. The Inquisitor, Fray Alonso de Peralta, was responsible for inflicting exceedingly cruel tortures on different members of the family. He extracted confessions from the governor's sister, Dona Francisca de Carvajal, her three daughters, Isabel, Catalina, and Leonor and young Luis de Carvajal. Cohen records that at one point during his sentencing young Luis was asked, "'Do you know, Luis, what the Inquisition and Holy Office really is?' To this Luis shouted in Latin, 'The council of the wicked and the seat of pestilence.' Then he added pathetically, 'Is there a worse torture in the world than for a man to have his hands tied and be surrounded by rabid dogs?'"[12]

The Carvajal family paid the ultimate price for secretly practicing their religion. On December 8, 1596, a great auto de fé
was held. Dona Francisca and her daughters were dressed in
the yellow sackcloths, the Sanbenitos, and paraded through
the town along with her son, Luis. They were marched to the
stakes but, in the end, they were reconciled with the Church
so that they would be saved from death by fire, strangled
first before their bodies were consigned to the flames. Luis,
however, was to die a martyr, the flames taking his life. Four
years later, Luis's youngest sister, Mariana, was also condemned but she, like her mother and sisters, reconciled
herself with the Church, and she too was strangled before
her body was consigned to the flames. Governor Carvajal
had never denounced his family before the tribunal and for
his collusion, he was stripped of his governorship and died in
prison.[13]

The Inquisition was established in Lima, Peru in 1570
and the autos de fé were carried out there as well. In 1626,
five Marranos died at the stake. Roth points out that in the
last quarter of the sixteenth century in the New World alone,
"no fewer than 879 trials had taken place, activity being thus
nearly as great as that of the far-famed tribunal of Toledo."[14]
In the early seventeenth century, in Lima, Peru, a secret
group of practicing Jews called the Complicidad Grande met
often at the home of Manuel Bautista Perez. The group was
denounced before the Peruvian Inquisition, and on January
23, 1639, eleven men and women died as martyrs.[15] Cohen
observes that, "in the two and a half centuries of its exis-
tence the Inquisition in New Spain had done its work well
against the children of Abraham. It had sent over a hundred
alleged Judaizers to their death, put scores of others to
flight, many of them among the most prominent citizens of

New Spain, and had frightened countless others into unswerving conformity to the church."[16] The Inquisition had grown so powerful in the New World that finally the Marranos were in as much jeopardy in the New World as they had been in the Old.

The story was much the same in Portuguese Brazil when in 1625, fourteen men and women were denounced before the Inquisition. Two people were burned at the stake and then historic events greatly impacted upon the Jews. Between 1624 and 1625 the Dutch attacked and seized Pernambuco, Brazil. The Dutch had been under Spanish rule and now, throwing off the yoke of Spain's dominance, they successfully captured Pernambuco and strengthened their position in the New World. The Dutch quickly opened the Netherlands to the Jews, who, because of the Inquisition, were considered enemies of Spain and Portugal. Hundreds of Marranos fled to the Netherlands and proclaimed their Judaism. Many sailed to the Dutch territories in the New World. The Jews proved to be trusted allies for the Dutch. Nuno Alvarez Franco and Manuel Fernandez Drago, Antonio Vaez Henriquez (Moses Cohen), and David Peixotto helped the Dutch capture Bahia, Pernambuco, and the Island of Fernando de Noronha.[17] When in 1630 the Dutch won Recife, they again proclaimed religious freedom for the Marranos living there. By 1640 a large Jewish community was flourishing in Recife. The Jews were very successful traders, particularly in sugar, but they were also active in the spice, salt, wine, fruit, dyewood (used in textiles), indigo, tobacco, silver, and gold trades.[18] Their goods were exchanged in Amsterdam for basic supplies, such as flour, bread, and beer, as well as for luxury items such as silk and books.

In Amsterdam the Jews rose quickly to become prominent citizens, actively trading with their brethren in the New
World. Some Jews became brokers in the diamond trade,
and were involved in every aspect of the industry, working as
dealers, cutters, and polishers. A number of Jews also became shipowners, importers, and exporters. As a result of
solid backing from the Amsterdam Jews, the Sephardic
community in Recife had grown to 600 people by 1642, and
they were able to bring Isaac Aboab de Fonseca to officiate
as a rabbi in the New World.[19] When Recife was recaptured
by the Portuguese in 1654, the Dutch, under the command
of Sigismund Schoppe, insisted that the Jews be assured
safe passage. Many of the Jews chose to sail back to Amsterdam, including Rabbi Fonseca. However, twenty-three
Jews sailed for New Amsterdam. Some of these first colonial
North American Jews were: Asser Levy, Abram and David
Israel, Mose Lumbroso, the widows Judith de Mercado,
Ricke Nunes and their families. They departed Recife on a
ship called the *Falcon*, which sailed into a raging storm,
hurtling them towards Spanish Jamaica. Many of these Jews
had narrowly escaped the Inquisition in Portugal so that
when they landed in Spanish territory they were once again
in serious jeopardy. The Spanish authorities took them into
custody but the Dutch West Indies Company protested their
treatment and secured their release.

It is interesting to note that there was a subtle difference
in Church policy in Jamaica than in other Spanish colonies.
Queen Isabella had promised Columbus that, "no branch of
the Holy Office was to be established in lands under his
dominion."[20] Columbus's property rights to Jamaica were
established by his son Diego in 1506 and again in 1538.[21]
Why did Isabella refrain from establishing the Inquisition

in lands under Columbus's domain? While the question once again must go unanswered, it again suggests that Columbus was of Jewish extraction, that his family may have been practicing Jews, and that Isabella was aware of this.

Once released, the twenty-three Jews booked passage on the *St. Charles*, which took them safely from Jamaica to New Amsterdam. After their long, arduous journey, Governor Peter Stuyvesant received them with hostility. Stuyvesant felt the Jews would be a burden to the young colony and wrote to the Company in the harshest words.

> The Jews who have arrived would nearly all like to remain here, but learning that they (with their customary usury and deceitful trading with the Christians) were repugnant to the inferior magistrates, as also to the people having the most affection for you; the Deaconry also fearing that owing to their present indigence they might become a charge in the coming winter, we have, for the benefit of this weak and newly developing land, deemed it useful to require them in a friendly way to depart; praying . . . that the deceitful race—such hateful blasphemers of the name of Christ—be not allowed further to infect and trouble this new colony, to the detraction of your worships and the dissatisfaction of your worships' most affectionate subjects.[22]

Stuyvesant's complaints were made in vain. The Dutch West Indies Company had a number of influential Jews as stockholders, and they convinced the Company to allow the Jews to remain. The Company replied:

It is well known to your Honors that the Jewish nation
in Brazil have at all times been faithful and have striven
to guard and maintain that place risking for that purpose their possessions and their blood.

Yonder land is extensive and spacious. The more of
loyal people that go to live there, the better it is in
regard to the population of the country as in regard to
the payment of various excises and taxes which may be
imposed there, and in regard to the increase of trade,
and also to the importation of all the necessaries that
may be sent there.

Your Honors should also consider that the Honorable
Lords, the Burgomasters of the City, and the Honorable High Illustrious Mighty Lords, the States-General,
have in political matters always protected and considered the Jewish nation as upon the same footing as all
the inhabitants and burghers . . .

Your Honors should also please consider that many of
the Jewish nation are principal shareholders in the
Company.[23]

Forced to accept the Jews in New Amsterdam, Stuyvesant
tried to deny them many of the rights granted to the other
colonists. The Jews were forbidden to purchase homes,
practice a craft, sell at retail, trade with outlying settlements
and Indians, stand guard with the militiamen, practice public
worship, vote, and hold public office.[24] During the next ten
years, the Jews managed to acquire many of these rights,
fighting numerous battles in court and suffering imprison-
ment in order to receive payment for goods, the right to
establish businesses and trade, the right to establish a religious congregation, and even the right to stand guard with

the militiamen. Once these rights were established, the Jews were involved in commerce and trade. They were active in such occupations as tallow chandlers, watchmakers, soapmakers, saddlers, bakers, shoemakers, wigmakers, engravers, snuff makers, distillers, indigo sorters, braziers, and silversmiths.[25] They were also doctors and butchers. Along with Jacob Barsimson and Solomon Pietersen, Jews who were already in New Amsterdam, the Sephardic Jews established the congregation, Shearith Israel or Remnant of Israel, in the year 1654, the first Jewish congregation in North America. By the time the British captured New Amsterdam in 1664, the Jewish colonists were an integral part of the Dutch community.

Sephardic congregations began to sprout throughout the Caribbean. In 1650 the congregation Nidhe Israel, Dispersed of Israel, was established in English Barbados and Rabbi David Sarfatty de Pina braved the New World to serve this congregation. In 1654 on the Dutch island of Curacao Hope of Israel was established. In 1674 Rabbi Haham Josiao Pardo arrived to serve that congregation.[26]

From the most humble beginnings of Luis de Torres speaking Hebrew to the Arawak people, the Sephardic Jews came to the New World, seeking religious freedom. Though we cannot ascertain whether Columbus intentionally set out to find a land where the Jews could escape the fires of the Inquisition, we do know that he discovered a New World where religious freedom ultimately conquered the prejudices of the Old.

16

COLUMBUS'S JEWISH ROOTS: THE EVIDENCE

Portrait of Columbus in his later years, attributed to Ghirlandaio.

Who was Christopher Columbus, and what was the driving force behind his dream to discover a western route to the Indies? Was it a desire to find a peaceful land for the Jews or was it a quest to carve his name into history, to be the first explorer to conquer the unknown western ocean sea? Certainly he was a complicated man, driven to some extent by fanatic religious feelings that seem to have been influenced by a mixture of Judaeo-Christian doctrine. The mysteries surrounding Columbus's life cause many scholars to question his origin, his extraction, and his unspoken but deeply felt motives. Certainly Columbus's life was intertwined with the Jews of Spain and Portugal. In his unrelenting search for a sponsor for the enterprise, he placed such pressure on the Spanish Crown that it may have been the catalyst in the decision to expel the Jews. But his discovery of a New World ultimately gave the Jews a land where they could live in peace.

A close examination of Columbus's life causes some of the mysteries to fade, and the man begins to move out of the shadows he so carefully cast about him. The fact that his name was Cristobal Colon simply cannot be ignored. The name Colon, which his son Ferdinand documented as being the original family name, has a rich Hebraic origin. It means Jonah or dove and, as Roth documents, was the original name used by Italian Jews who called themselves Colombo. Madariaga notes that some Jews who survived the 1391 massacres in Catalonia eventually made their way into the Italian city states, explaining how the Colons found their way to Genoa. The fact that Columbus's father was a weaver also lends credence to the idea that the family was of Jewish extraction. Weaving was one of the few occupations open to Jews, and while it does not prove that the Colombo family was Jewish, it is important to note that they made their living in an occupation open to the Jews.

Columbus led a colorful life on the high seas even before he was 20 years old. In his writings, he told of how he had been a corsair captain and had tricked his men into attacking the Aragonese ship the *Fernandina* in 1472. It was interesting that he would confide such a thing in a letter to King Ferdinand, for not only was the *Fernandina* named after Ferdinand but Columbus was sailing for King Rene d'Anjou, the archenemy of Ferdinand's father. This fact, along with others dealing with Columbus's relationship to Casenove-Coullon, led Madariaga to question which side Columbus was on in the 1476 sea battle off Cape St. Vincent. If Columbus was with the French rather than the Genoese, then his allegiance would suggest a Spanish-Jewish extraction. Morison surmises that Columbus was with the seamen from Savona on the ship *Bechalla,* part of the Genoese convoy. But Morison ignores Columbus's statement that he had been a captain at a young age and would probably not have been a common sailor when he was 25. Even Morison concedes that Columbus's name was not on any of the *Bechalla's* lists, so it is conceivable that Columbus was with the attacking French fleet.

Madariaga's suggestion that Columbus was sailing with the admiral of the French fleet, Casenove-Coullon, seems credible. Columbus sailed with the French in 1472 so it was quite possible that he was with the French in 1476. In further support of this argument is the fact that Columbus claimed to have an admiral in his family. Cecil Roth points out that the Jewish Colon–Colombo families in northern Italy were related to the French as well as to the Spanish Catalonians. The name Coullon is translated Colombo in Italian and Colon in Spanish. It is possible that Casenove-Coullon was the admiral Columbus was related to, and the admiral he sailed with during the 1476 sea battle.

The last point that suggests that Columbus was with the French rather than the Genoese is that he washed ashore with the French and did not sail to Cadiz with the Genoese. What was a Genoese seaman doing with the French? If Columbus was of Jewish extraction, related to Casenove-Coullon, he probably would have been with the French fleet. The French had been at war with the Aragonese for the province of Roussillon, and the Catalonian Jews would have sided with the French, since it was the Aragonese who had rioted against them. Perhaps the Catalonian Jews dreamt of returning to Catalonia. It might very well have been the desire of the Columbus family, for it seems they spoke Castilian in their home.

It was evident that Columbus spoke and wrote in an old Castilian and not Italian. Morison suggests that Columbus could have learned his Castilian from the Genoese living in Portugal but again Madariaga offers a different explanation. He suggests that if the Columbus family had originated from Catalonia, then the language used at home would have been an old Castilian. Cecil Roth also points out that in Columbus's notes in the margins of his books, his Latin mistakes show that he was thinking in Castilian and not Italian. Therefore it has been surmised that Castilian was his first language.

Once Columbus landed in Portugal, his life became more overtly intertwined with the Jews. We know he made numerous trips to one of three Juderias in Lisbon because he left money to the gatekeeper in his will. During this period Columbus may have met Don Isaac Abravanel, treasurer to King Afonso V. Perhaps this was his reason for going so often to the Juderias. It was Abravanel who eventually helped finance the first voyage.

In the 1470s Portugal was in the forefront of exploration. Prince Henry the Navigator had established his navigation academy in Sagres where outstanding astronomers, mathematicians, and cartographers were assembled. Prince Henry brought together three great Jewish scholars, Mestre Jaime, Mestre Joseph Vizinho and Abraham Zacuto, and it is clear that Columbus was acquainted with their work.

Columbus took full advantage of this seafaring kingdom, sailing south to Africa and then north to England and Iceland. In 1478 Columbus made a voyage for the Genoese merchants Ludavico Centurione and Paolo Di Negro. It has been noted that the Di Negro family was a well known Portuguese Jewish family. It has not been established, however, if Paolo Di Negro was a member of the Jewish Di Negro family, but if he had been, then Columbus was working for this powerful Jewish family very early in his career.

Columbus made an excellent match when he married Dona Felipa Perestrello in 1479. She was of noble birth and her family's estates included part of the island of Porto Santo, one of the Madeira Islands. These were the islands the explorers passed on their way to Africa. Taking up residence on Porto Santo, Columbus made a study of his late father-in-law's charts and began to keep records of the Atlantic trade winds. He also used this time to gather as much information as he could concerning the lands west of the Ocean Sea. The information he collected contributed to the success of his historic voyage.

When King Afonso V died in 1481, Joao II (King John II) inherited his father's throne. Joao was dedicated to continuing his great-uncle Prince Henry's legacy of navigational superiority and extended exploration down the African coast. But Joao was also intent upon consolidating his power and his ruthless elimination of the princes of Braganza impacted upon the Jews of Portugal. Fernando, duke of Braganza, was Don Isaac Abravanel's closest friend and ally. When the duke was arrested for high treason, Don Isaac was forced to flee into Spain. Don Isaac had been the chief spokesperson for the Jews and with his fall, life for the Jews in Portugal became severely restricted. Rules and ordinances that had been rescinded during the reign of Afonso V were reinstated under King Joao II.

In 1481, Columbus finally obtained an audience with King Joao in which he presented his proposal to sail west in order to reach the East. The king's Advisory Committee figured that Columbus's calculations were far too short, and his proposal was rejected. However, Joao was willing to allow two other men, Fernao Dulmo and Joao Estreito, to try the expedition, since they would be able to finance it themselves. The king had nothing to lose and everything to gain, but Dulmo and Estreito did not have Columbus's knowledge of the trade winds. Their failure occurred because they could not fight the fierce trade winds they encountered off the Azores. Columbus was careful not to make that same mistake.

Disheartened by the king's rejection as well as by the death of his wife, Dona Felipa, Columbus left Portugal with his small son, Diego, for Spain. Though he blamed the Portuguese rejection on "the Court Jews," it was the Jews and Conversos in the Spanish Court who provided the critical support Columbus needed to convince Ferdinand and Isabella to back his enterprise.

When Columbus arrived in Spain in 1484, the reconquista of Moorish Granada was well underway. King Ferdinand and Queen Isabella were determined to oust the Moors and unite all of the Spains into one Christendom. The Jews were instrumental in helping raise funds for the reconquista. Abraham Seneor and Don Isaac Abravanel had become the monarchs' most trusted treasurers. But the reconquista would not benefit the Jews, for the Golden Age they had experienced under Moorish rule was coming to an end. Under the Moors, the great physician–theologian Maimonides lived until he and his family were forced to flee to Egypt, where he wrote the *Guide to the Perplexed*. The poets Solomon Ibn Gabirol and Judah HaLevi gave voice to the yearning for Jerusalem. The Jews had become an integral part of Spain. Even the names of great cities such as Toledo may have had Hebrew derivations. But seemingly unaware of their impending danger, the Jews helped the Catholic Monarchs defeat the Moors. The Monarchs' policy of a united church and state would ultimately be as devastating for the Jews as it was for the Moors.

Two years after Columbus arrived in Spain, he was granted an audience with the king and queen, and then spent the next six years petitioning them to grant him his expedition. Ferdinand and Isabella clearly were interested in his proposal, but the war in Granada was their first priority.

Columbus found that some of his strongest supporters were the Conversos within the Court, the king's treasurers, Luis de Santangel and Gabriel Sanchez. Indeed, Columbus's first letters on his voyage were addressed to these men. Other influential Conversos were Alonso de Cabrera and Pedro de la Caballeria, who had helped arrange Isabella's marriage to Ferdinand. The king's great-grandmother was from the Jewish Henriquez family, so it was not surprising that Columbus was surrounded with Conversos and men of Jewish extraction. And, it must be noted, life under the Inquisition was not safe for any of these men. Both Santangel and Sanchez were under constant surveillance from the Inquisition since members of their families had been burned at the stake for their part in the plot to murder Fray Pedro Arbues, the ruthless Inquisitor in Aragon.

But the Inquisition was targeting the secret Jews, the Marranos, who were actively practicing their religion in underground sanctuaries. The specific aim of the tribunals was to root out heresy within the Church, to find the newly converted who professed to believe in Catholicism but who secretly relapsed and practiced Judaism. When King Ferdi-

nand and Queen Isabella petitioned Pope Sixtus IV to expand the work of the Inquisition in 1478, an unprecedented
reign of terror was unleashed throughout the Spains. The
Marranos were tortured into confessing that their beloved
family members were heretics. Once the Church had such
confessions, the Marranos underwent the harsh penitence
of marching naked from the waist up or humiliatingly clad in
Sanbenitos in autos de fé processions. If they were not
reconciled with the Church, they were condemned to die a
fiery death. When the plague broke out in 1481, the terrified
population blamed the Jews. In a desperate effort to stop the
Inquisition from sending Jews to the stake, Diego Susan
conspired against the Inquisitors. His daughter gave the plan
away, and Susan, along with other conspirators, died in the
auto de fé they had tried so hard to stop.

With the appointment of Tomas Torquemada, an even
more virulent reign of terror was unleashed against the
Jews. Using his influence over the king and queen, Torquemada created an Inquisition that became an almost un-
controllable force. Roth estimates that during the three centuries in which it existed, the Inquisition was responsible for
more than 30,000 deaths. It was no wonder, then, that
during this time of tribulation any Christian of Jewish extraction would have been extremely careful to hide his family's
roots. Since Columbus so closely guarded his past, a
number of scholars believe he was hiding his Jewish extraction. When the Colom family in Catalonia was burned at the
stake in 1489, one wonders what impact this might have had
on Columbus. He had used the name Colom while living in
Portugal but reverted to Colon when in Spain because he felt
it was a safer name, as indeed it was.

On January 2, 1492, Boabdil, the last caliph to sit upon

the throne in Alhambra, surrendered to King Ferdinand and Queen Isabella. Shortly after this surrender, Columbus once more presented himself in Court but was refused because the Crown lacked funds. Within hours of this formal refusal, he was recalled and granted his expedition. What transpired during those crucial hours that changed the monarchs' minds and the course of history? It seems King Ferdinand's dilemma was twofold. His first problem, or crisis, was to keep Columbus from going to King Charles in France, Ferdinand's archenemy. Ferdinand did not want Charles to have a direct sea route to the Indies. Second, Ferdinand did not want a watered-down percentage of any profits, should Columbus succeed. The duke of Medinaceli was prepared to finance Columbus but then Ferdinand would have had a smaller percentage of the profit. Some scholars assert that most of the monies for the expedition came from the duke of Medinaceli. But most scholars agree that it was Luis de Santangel who convinced Ferdinand and Isabella that there would be enough funds for Columbus's voyage. Santangel must have known that Abravanel and Seneor would try to raise enough money to buy security for the Jews, enough money to finance Columbus. But even though Abravanel and Seneor did not perceive any immediate threat, it appears the edict to expel the Jews was already under serious consideration. King Ferdinand knew that monies confiscated from Jewish property would go a long way to paying off war debts as well as financing Columbus's expedition. Ferdinand was determined to have Columbus sail under the Spanish flag, and so he was granted his expedition. When the edict to expel the Jews was issued on March 30, 1492, Abravanel and Seneor were thrust into a desperate race to raise enough money to appease the king and have the edict rescinded.

The religious fanaticism of Queen Isabella cannot be ignored or discounted. Horrified over the trumped-up accusations concerning the La Guardia case, Isabella felt that the Jews must be expelled. However, when Abravanel and Seneor arrived in Alhambra with 30,000 ducats in hand and a promise of 300,000 more ducats, Ferdinand was prepared to rescind the edict. At that moment Tomas Torquemada dramatically appeared, scolded the monarchs and then threw a cross that hit Isabella in the head; the fate of the Spanish Jews was sealed. Ferdinand and Isabella would not defy Torquemada, and they let the edict stand.

And so as Columbus prepared to venture forth on his historic voyage, the Jews of Spain were wrenched from a land they had lived in for over a thousand years. Desperate efforts were made to find vessels to carry approximately 150,000 Jews to Naples, Corfu, Turkey, and North Africa. Many of the Jews who left on August 2, 1492, were sold into slavery by the unscrupulous sea captains who had taken money for their safe passage. Others suffered from starvation and the plague. Approximately 150,000 Jews made their way into Portugal, but those Jews were faced with expulsion and mass conversions. Don Isaac Abravanel and his family were among the more fortunate, finding a temporary safe haven in Naples. Circumstances were so desperate for the Jews that one must wonder if Columbus had a hidden agenda in his dream to reach the East by sea. As Simon Wiesenthal suggests, perhaps Columbus hoped to find a safe haven for the Jews.

On August 3, one day after the Jewish expulsion, Columbus set sail. It certainly was possible that Columbus sympathized with the Jews, for in his first letter to the king and queen, he made reference to the expulsion with no adulation for the action. No one can be certain as to his innermost thoughts, but even if Columbus had not set out to find a peaceful haven for the Jewish exiles, the Conversos on board certainly must have had this in mind. After a two-month crossing, at early dawn, October 12, 1492, the sailor Rodrigo de Triana, who some claim was also a Converso, cried out that he saw land.

When Columbus first encountered the Arawak people he was greeted as a "man from heaven," but he viewed them as a potential source of free labor. Though Isabella abhorred the idea of impressing the Arawak people into slavery, she accepted slaves if they were taken in battle. She had taken Moorish slaves with the fall of Malaga. Like disease, slavery was an evil carried from the Old World to the New. In the Old World white slave trade was still very much in evidence throughout the Mediterranean area. Many of the Jewish slaves were rescued by their brethren in foreign lands. The Bahama Arawak people had no one to save them, and they did not survive their enslavement.

After two months of exploration, Columbus's flag ship, the *Santa Maria*, was stranded on Christmas Eve in a place he named La Navidad, Hispaniola. He left behind most of her crew in the rugged fort they built, and then, laden with spices, parrots, gold, and native people, Columbus sailed back to Spain. When he arrived he was hailed as the first European to cross the Ocean Sea and to open a water route to the Indies.

Between the years 1492 and 1504 Columbus made four voyages to the New World, his talents resting in his navigational abilities. Much of the money for these voyages came from the confiscated properties of the expelled Jews. Though the Santa Fe Capitulations designated Columbus as the governor and viceroy-general, he did not have the ability to govern the vast territories he discovered. He was inconsistent in his treatment of his men and the native people. Sometimes he was too lenient when it was necessary to show strength but more often he was too brutal over minor infractions. His severest critics, however, came from the clergy who accompanied him on these voyages. His poor judgment in cutting off Fray Buil's food supply cost him dearly when that friar reported back to Ferdinand and Isabella. It is interesting to note that Columbus and his brothers were referred to as Conversos in the New World. If Columbus had been of Jewish descent, and the Spaniards were aware of it, then his ability to govern them would have been extremely difficult, as indeed it seems to have been. There is some speculation that the secret code the Columbus brothers used in writing to one another may have been Hebrew script. But whatever the underlying cause for lack of strong leadership was, we know Columbus was continuously fighting rebellions. The situation deteriorated so badly that King Ferdinand and Queen Isabella's emissary, Francisco de Bobadilla, arrived in Hispaniola, arrested Columbus and his brothers, and then sent them back to Spain. It was the most humiliating time in Columbus's life.

It is clear that at this time as well as throughout his life, Columbus was greatly influenced by the Old Testament. Some scholars suggest that his numerous Judaic references give significant insight into Columbus's religious orientation. These scholars are referring to notes written in the margins of his books in Columbus's hand that were never intended for others to see. His journal had a significant number of Judaic references to Abraham, Isaac, Moses, and David. His journal also revealed his obsession to liberate Jerusalem. In fact his main objective for finding a route to the Indies was to return to Spain with enough gold to finance a crusade. But the most interesting fact to come to light was Columbus's dating of the destruction of the Second Temple in Jerusalem. His date was based on Jewish reckoning rather than Christian.

The fourth voyage to the New World proved to be Columbus's greatest test as a navigator and seaman, for he was constantly buffeted by raging storms that weakened even his toughest sailors. Often lashing himself to impro-vised deck quarters, he explored Panama and Costa Rica, looking for a strait leading to the Pacific Ocean. Once he was convinced that no such strait existed, he began his success-ful search for gold. Near the end of his exploration his wooden ships were so rotted by barnacles and worms that they barely stayed afloat, forcing Columbus to sail for Ja-maica where they were beached. Stranded on the island and surrounded by hostile native people, Columbus sent his most trusted friend, Diego Mendez, off in a large canoe to seek help in Hispaniola. While Columbus was marooned, he began signing his name in the curious triangular fashion that some scholars suggest was a subterfuge for the triangular Star of David. It has been suggested that the signature served as a secret supplication to God, a blessing Columbus wished to pass on to his sons, for he insisted that his sons use this signature in perpetuity.

Columbus also marked the upper lefthand corner of his personal letters to his son, Diego. The one letter to Diego, which was also intended for Ferdinand and Isabella, was missing this mark. It has been suggested that the marking may have been the Hebrew letters Bet Heh, which were often used as a Jewish symbol for the blessing, "With the help of God." While these markings may have been nothing more than some notation from a library in which the letters were stored, it must be noted that the Jews in the fifteenth century did place a Bet Heh in the upper lefthand corner of their letters.

It is also curious to note that once Columbus sailed back to Seville and began to make out his last will and testament, he made three provisions that add additional support to the supposition that Columbus was of Jewish extraction. Columbus wished to provide money for the poor, an old Jewish custom called tithing; he wanted to provide a dowry for poor girls; and he wished to remember the Jew who lived at the entrance to a Lisbon Juderia. It is possible that at the end of his life, Columbus did not want to forget some of the cherished customs of his forefathers.

The legacy Columbus left to the Jews of Spain and Portugal was a rugged New World to which they could flee. Marranos settled in some of the earliest outposts in New Spain. However, in 1511 Queen Isabella's daughter, Queen Juana, established the Inquisition in Hispaniola. Over the next two centuries, more than one hundred men, women, and children were burned at the stake in the New World. But other factors began to reshape the New World. When the Dutch colonies were established in 1625, the Jews finally were able to practice their religion as their forefathers had done for centuries. With the fall of Dutch Recife back into the hands of the Portuguese in 1654, a small but hardy group of twenty-three men, women, and children traveled north to New Amsterdam. Though Peter Stuyvesant gave them a hostile reception, the Dutch West Indies Company insisted that the Jews be allowed to stay and be treated like the other Dutch colonists. Jewish communities began to flourish from the mid 1600s throughout the Caribbean and North America.

Christopher Columbus, or Cristobal Colon, was an enigmatic character. The possibility exists that the mysteries surrounding his life were put in place specifically for the purpose of hiding his Jewish extraction from the Inquisition at a time when such an identity could have sent him to the stake. Indeed, a Colom family died in an auto de fé in Catalonia, the land where Madariaga believed Columbus's family may have originated. A number of issues, such as his family name, Colon, the fact that the Colons were weavers, his possible relation to Admiral Casenove-Coullon, his facility with the Castilian language, his close relationships to the Conversos at the Spanish Court, the ultimate financial backing for his enterprise from Abravanel, his constant Judaic references to Moses, the Jewish kings and prophets, his unusual triangular signature and special markings at the top of his personal letters, his dating of the destruction of the Second Temple in Jerusalem, and his overwhelming desire to liberate Jerusalem all lead one to believe that he may have lived a double life. While ostensibly he was a Catholic, his private world seems to have been deeply influenced by Judaism. Columbus was a pragmatist. The world in which he found himself dictated that he stifle any facts concerning his past that would have jeopardized his proposal to sail west. If he had been of Jewish extraction, he would have had to hide any linkage to that extraction from the eyes of the Inquisition and make a great show of his Catholicism. In fact, he may have been a deeply religious Catholic even if he had been of Jewish extraction. The one supposition does not necessarily negate the other. Many Conversos were devout Catholics while also cherishing aspects of their Judaism.

Though substantial evidence points to the very real possibility that Columbus was of Jewish extraction, his Jewish roots are yet to be established with certainty. However, his contribution to the survival of the Jewish people cannot be underestimated. At a time when intolerance had reached a fevered pitch, Columbus opened a New World to which the Jews could flee from the religious persecution of the Old. With great perseverance and courage, the Jews ultimately won the right to practice their religion in the New World Columbus discovered.

APPENDIX: CHRONOLOGY

The following chronology highlights a number of significant individuals and related events that impacted upon Christopher Columbus and the Jews of Spain.

100–170: Ptolemy flourishes in Alexandria.

711: The Moors invade Spain under Djabal at-Tarik.

1063: King Sancho Ramirez of Aragon begins the reconquista.

1135–1204: Maimonides lives in Spain and Egypt.

1391: Riots take place against the Jews in Catalonia and throughout the Spains.

April of 1451: Queen Isabella is born in Castile.

Fall of 1451: Columbus is born in Genoa.

1456: Prince Henry the Navigator is granted papal permission to explore the Gold and Ivory Coasts of Africa.

1469: Ferdinand and Isabella are married in Castile.

1472: Columbus sails as a corsair for King Rene d'Anjou.

June 25, 1474: Prince Joao of Portugal receives a letter from Toscanelli indicating that one could sail west to reach the East.

1474: King Enrique's death in Castile precipitates the Spanish-Portuguese War.

August 13, 1476: Columbus lands in Portugal after the battle off Cape St. Vincent.

1477: Columbus sails to England and Iceland.

November 1, 1478: Pope Sixtus IV issues a bull to expand the Inquisition in the Spains.

1479: Columbus marries Dona Felipa Perestrello.

1479: Diego Columbus is born.

1481: King Afonso of Portugal is succeeded by Joao II.

1481: The plague leads to a drastic increase in autos de fé in the Spains.

1483: Don Isaac Abravanel flees Portugal for Spain.

October 17, 1483: Tomas Torquemada is appointed Grand Inquisitor of the Spanish Inquisition.

1484: Columbus is granted an audience with King Joao but the Royal Committee rejects his proposal.

1484: Columbus arrives in Spain with his son Diego.

1485: Fray Pedro Arbues is assassinated in Saragossa.

1486: Columbus is granted an audience with Ferdinand and Isabella.

1487: Bartholomew Diaz rounds the Cape of Good Hope.

1489: Coloms die at the stake in Tarragona.

November 14, 1491: Four men are condemned in the La Guardia trial and burned at the stake.

January 2, 1492: Boabdil the Young surrenders Alhambra to King Ferdinand and Queen Isabella.

March 30, 1492: The Edict to Expel the Jews is issued.

April 30, 1492: The Edict to Expel the Jews is publicly announced along with Columbus's orders to equip a fleet.

August 2, 1492: The Jewish mass exodus from Spain takes place.

August 3, 1492: Columbus sets sail on his first historic voyage.

October 12, 1492: Land is discovered.

March 31, 1493: Columbus leads a triumphant procession from Palos to Seville.

September 25, 1493: Columbus sets out on his second expedition.

May 30, 1498: Columbus begins his third expedition from which he returns bound in iron chains.

April 3, 1502: Columbus begins his fourth and final voyage.

November 7, 1504: Columbus arrives back in Spain.

May 20, 1506: After making his will, Columbus dies.

1509: King Ferdinand allows Conversos to emigrate to the New World for the price of 20,000 ducats.

1511: Queen Juana establishes the Inquisition in New Spain.

1518: Autos de fé are carried out in Hispaniola.

1570: The Inquisition is established in Lima, Peru.

December 8, 1596: Several members of Governor Carvajal's family die in an auto de fé in Mexico.

1630: The Dutch win Recife from the Portuguese and proclaim religious freedom for the Marranos.

1654: The Dutch lose Recife from the Portuguese and twenty-three Jews arrive in New Amsterdam.

ENDNOTES

Chapter 1

1. Salvador de Madariaga, *Christopher Columbus: Being the Life of the Very Magnificent Lord Don Cristobal Colon* (New York: Macmillan, 1940), p. 183.

2. Samuel Eliot Morison, *Admiral of the Ocean Sea* (Boston: Little, Brown, 1942), p. 7.

3. Ibid.

4. Cecil Roth, *A History of the Marranos* (New York: Schocken Books, 1974), pp. 14–15.

5. Ibid, p. 15.

6. Yitzhak Baer, *A History of the Jews in Christian Spain* (Philadelphia: The Jewish Publication Society), p. 110.

7. Madariaga, p. 57.

8. Cecil Roth, *Personalities and Events in Jewish History* (Philadelphia: The Jewish Publication Society), p. 203.

9. Ibid., p. 202.

10. Morison, p. 9.

Chapter 2

1. Morison, p. 23.

2. Madariaga, p. 40.

3. Morison, p. 23.

4. Ibid., p. 20.

5. M. Kayserling, *Christopher Columbus and the Participation of the Jews in the Spanish and Portuguese Discoveries* (New York: Hermon Press, 1968), p. 1.

6. Ibid., pp. 2, 5–6.

7. Madariaga, p. 65.

8. Roth, *Personalities*, p. 204.

9. Madariaga, p. 48.

10. Ibid.

Chapter 3

1. Madariaga, p. 76.

2. Ibid., p. 77.

3. Ibid., p. 56.

4. Ibid,

5. Roth, *Personalities*, p. 196.

6. Ibid., p. 197.

Chapter 4

1. Morison, p. 31.

2. Ibid., p. 24.

3. Ibid., p. 25.

4. Ibid., p. 41.

5. Madariaga, p. 89.

6. Ibid., p. 88.

7. Morison, p. 65.

8. Ibid., p. 71.

9. Ibid., p. 68.

10. Ibid., p. 74.

Chapter 5

1. Eliyahu Ashtor, *The Jews of Moslem Spain*, vol. I (Philadelphia: The Jewish Publication Society, 1984), p. 9.

2. Madariaga, p. 119.

3. Ashtor, "Return, O My Soul," vol. III, p. 42.

4. Israel Zinberg, "My heart is in the East," *A History of Jewish Literature: The Arabic Spanish Period* (Philadelphia: The Jewish Publication Society, 1972), p. 95.

5. B. Netanyahu, *Don Isaac Abravanel: Statesman and Philosopher* (Philadelphia: The Jewish Publication Society, 1972), p. 48.

Chapter 6

1. Madariaga, p. 144.

2. Ibid., p. 143.

3. Ibid., p. 151.

4. Roth, *Marranos*, p. 24.

5. Kayserling, p. 45.

6. Roth, *Marranos*, p. 81.

7. Madariaga, p. 154.

8. Ibid., p. 150.

9. Roth, *Marranos*, p. 25.

10. Kayserling, p. 26.

11. Roth, *Marranos*, p. 51.

12. Madariaga, p. 173.

13. Kayserling, p. 29.

14. Roth, *Marranos*, p. 24.

15. Ibid., p. 50.

16. Ibid.

17. Walter F. McEntire, *Was Columbus a Jew?* (Boston: Stratford, 1925), p. 73.

18. Roth, *Marranos*, p. 51.

Chapter 7

1. Roth, *Marranos*, p. 124.

2. Ibid., p. 47.

3. Baer, vol. II, p. 306.

4. Ibid., p. 313.

5. Roth, *Marranos*, pp. 109–110.

6. Ibid., pp. 100–102.

7. Ibid., p. 42.

8. Ibid., p. 43–44.

9. Baer, p. 327.

10. Roth, *Marranos*, p. 145.

11. "Kol Nidrei," *Encyclopaedia Judaica*, vol. 10, p. 1167.

12. Madariaga, p. 60.

13. Ibid., p. 175.

Chapter 8

1. Madariaga, p. 160.

2. Ibid., p. 161.

3. Ibid., p. 175.

4. Ibid., p. 168.

5. Ibid.

6. Morison, p. 105.

7. Baer, vol. II, p. 421.

8. Ibid., p. 423.

9. Roth, *Marranos*, p. 52.

10. Kayserling, p. 83.

11. Ibid., p. 54.

12. Ibid., pp. 77–78.

13. Baer, p. 433.

14. Kayserling, pp. 85–86.

15. Madariaga, p. 188.

Chapter 9

1. "Edict of Expulsion," In E. H. Lindo, *The Jews of Spain and Portugal* (London: Longman, Brown, Green & Longmans, 1848), pp. 277–280.

2. Netanyahu, p. 55.

3. Joseph Sarchek, *Don Isaac Abravanel* (New York: Bloch, 1938), p. 43.

4. Netanyahu, p. 56.

5. Simon Noveck, *Great Jewish Personalties in Ancient & Medieval Times,* vol. I (Clinton, MA: B'nai B'rith Department of Adult Jewish Education, 1959), p. 268.

6. Baer, p. 436.

7. Ibid.

8. Noveck, pp. 269–270.

9. Robert Sugar, ed. *Journey of Fifteen Centuries* (New York: Union of American Hebrew Congregations, 1973), Section B.

10. Netanyahu, p. 57.

Chapter 10

1. Kayserling, p. 88.

2. Netanyahu, p. 61.

3. Ibid., p. 63.

4. Heinrich Graetz, *Popular History of the Jews,* vol. IV (New York: Jordan Publishing Company, 1935), p. 230.

5. Ibid., p. 231.

6. Ibid.

7. Simon Wiesenthal, *Sails of Hope* (New York: Macmillan, 1973), p. 234.

8. Morison, p. 138.

9. Ibid., p. 139.

10. Ibid., p. 142.

11. Kayserling, p. 190.

12. Morison, pp. 153–154.

13. Kayserling, p. 93.

14. Roth, *Marranos*, p. 272.

15. Kayserling, p. 92.

Chapter 11

1. Morison, pp. 228–229.

2. Ibid., pp. 229–230.

3. Ibid., p. 242.

4. Ibid., p. 250.

5. Ernle Bradford, *Christopher Columbus* (New York: Viking, 1971), pp. 127–128.

6. Ibid., p. 132.

7. William H. Prescott, *History of the Reign of Ferdinand and Isabella the Catholic* (Philadelphia: J. B. Lippincott, 1900), p. 434.

8. Madariaga, p. 296.

9. Graetz, p. 229.

10. Ibid., p. 230.

11. Jacob Marcus, *The Jew in the Medieval World* (Cincinnati, OH: Union of American Hebrew Congregations, 1938), p. 53.

12. Ibid., p. 54.

13. Ibid., p. 53.

14. Graetz, p. 240.

15. Bradford, pp. 142–143.

16. Ibid., p. 144.

Chapter 12

1. Madariaga, p. 244.

2. Ibid., p. 243.

3. Ibid., p. 244.

4. Morison, pp. 134–135.

5. Madariaga, p. 290.

6. Ibid.

7. Ibid., p. 329.

8. Ibid., p. 343.

9. Ibid., p. 349.

10. Ibid.

Chapter 13

1. Madariaga, p. 361.

2. Ibid.

3. Ibid., p. 93.

4. Ibid., p. 100.

5. Ibid.

6. Ibid.

7. Ibid., p. 183.

8. Ibid., p. 184.

9. Ibid., p. 206.

10. Morison, p. 171.

11. Madariaga, p. 216.

12. Morison, p. 279.

13. Madariaga, p. 327.

14. Morison, p. 304.

15. Madariaga, p. 369.

16. Ibid., p. 375.

17. Ibid., pp. 379–380.

18. Morison, p. 516.

19. Roth, *Personalities*, p. 206.

20. Ibid.

21. Ibid.

22. Ibid., p. 207.

Chapter 14

1. Madariaga, p. 353.

2. Morison, p. 590.

3. Ibid., pp. 597, 600.

4. Ibid., p. 659.

5. Roth, *Personalities*, p. 210.

6. Maurice David, *Who Was Columbus? His Real Name and Real Fatherland* (New York: The Research Publishing Company, 1933), pp. 97, 107.

7. Madariaga, p. 403.

8. Ibid.

9. David, p. 99.

10. Ibid., p. 103.

11. Ibid.

12. Ibid., p. 98.

13. Madariaga, p. 404.

14. David, p. 108.

15. Roth, *Personalities*, p. 210.

16. Ibid., p. 208.

17. David, p. 105.

18. Ibid., p. 107.

19. Ibid., p. 106.

20. Ibid., p. 118.

Chapter 15

1. Kayserling, p. 127.

2. Roth, *Marranos*, p. 273.

3. Ibid.

4. Kayserling, p. 128.

5. Roth, *Marranos*, p. 274.

6. Kayserling, p. 130.

7. Ibid., p. 133.

8. Ibid.

9. Seymour B. Liebman, *New World Jewry: Requiem for the Forgotten* (New York: Ktav Publishing Company, 1982), p. 110.

10. Martin A. Cohen, *The Martyr* (Philadelphia: The Jewish Publication Society, 1973), p. 69.

11. Ibid., p. 8.

12. Ibid., p. 257.

13. Roth, *Marranos*, pp. 276–277.

14. Ibid., p. 277.

15. Ibid., p. 279.

16. Cohen, p. 272.

17. Roth, *Marranos*, p. 285.

18. Arnold Wiznitzer, *Jews in Colonial Brazil* (New York: Columbia University Press, 1960), p. 43.

19. Paul Masserman and Max Baker, *The Jews Come to America* (New York: Bloch, 1932), p. 24.

20. Liebman, p. 178.

21. Ibid.

22. Kenneth Libo and Irving Howe, *We Lived There Too* (New York: St. Martin's/Marek, 1984), p. 41.

23. Ibid., p. 42.

24. Jacob R. Marcus, *Early American Jewry*, vol. II (New York: Ktav, 1955), p. 384.

25. Ibid., p. 397.

26. Liebman, pp. 176–177.

GLOSSARY

Alcalde Mayor—a Spanish term for chief magistrate.

Aragon—a northern region of Spain that at one time had been a petty kingdom, one of the several kingdoms of the Spains. This is where King Ferdinand was born.

Auto de fé—Act of Faith—refers to a procession of penitents, often leading to a public square where heretics found guilty by the Church were burned at the stake. The act of burning heretics was carried out by the secular law.

Cacique—the name for the chief of the native people Columbus encountered in the New World.

Cassava—a bread made from a starchy root found in the New World.

Castile—a central region in Spain that was the strongest of the kingdoms of the Spains. Queen Isabella was born in Castile.

Catalonia—a northeastern region in Spain. It has been speculated that the Colon family originated from Catalonia.

Cathay—Columbus's name for China in 1492.

Cipango—Columbus's name for Japan in 1492.

Contador Mayor—a Spanish term for Chief Treasurer and Accountant.

Converso—the term used for Jews who converted to Catholicism.

Corsair—a privateer often associated with pirating.

Escribano de Racion—the Spanish term for Minister of Budget.

Gold ducat—a denomination of money significantly larger than the copper maravedis. 30,000 gold ducats were offered as ransom for the Jews of Spain.

Hermandad—Queen Isabella's police force.

Hispaniola—the Spanish name for today's Haiti and Dominican Republic.

Historia Rerum Ubique Gestarum—(*A History of Events*) was written by Pope Pius II, born Aeneas Sylvius (1405–1464).

Imago Mundi—(*Image of the World*) was written by Cardinal Pierre d'Ailly (1350–1420) concerning the known inhabitable lands.

Judaizing—the act of a converted Jew practicing his former religion. It was considered a heresy within the Catholic Church.

Juderia—the name for a Jewish ghetto in Spain and Portugal.

Maravedis—a Spanish denomination of money coined in copper. 2,000,000 Maravedis were needed to finance Columbus's voyage.

Marranos—a derogatory word meaning "pig," used for Jews who had converted to Catholicism but who secretly practiced Judaism.

Over the centuries it has become an ennobling name referring to the secret Jews who, under great duress, did not forsake their religion.

Mudejar—a lacy arched design used by the Moors in their doorways and windows.

Ocean Sea—also Western Ocean and Green Sea. Names used for the Atlantic Ocean in 1492.

Ptolemy—lived in Alexandria in 2 A.D. and theorized that the earth was the center of the universe. Columbus was one of the first great discoverers to question Ptolemy.

Quemadero—an area outside the city gates where the stakes for the autos de fé were arranged.

Relaxed to secular law—after the Inquisition's tribunal found a heretic guilty, the Church turned the heretic over to the secular law for punishment.

Sagres—the Portuguese center of navigational learning established by Prince Henry the Navigator in the 1400s.

Sanbenito—a yellow sack cloth painted with devils and flames. Heretics were forced to wear the Sanbenito in auto de fé processions.

Sephardim—the Jews (and their descendants) who were forced to flee Spain and Portugal in the 1490s.

Tax farmers—a term for royal tax collectors.

Tile—or Thule or Thyle—the name Columbus used for Iceland.

Torrid Zone—one of five zones considered to be uninhabitable before the great discoverers proved this theory wrong.

BIBLIOGRAPHY

Abrahams, I. (1958). *Jewish Life in the Middle Ages*. New York: Meridian Books.

Ashtor, E. (1984). *The Jews of Moslem Spain*. 3 vols. Philadelphia, PA: The Jewish Publication Society.

Baer, Y. (1966). *A History of the Jews in Christian Spain*. Philadelphia, PA: The Jewish Publication Society.

Baron, S. (1967). *A Social and Religious History of the Jews*. Vol. XI. New York: Columbia University Press.

Bradford, E. (1973). *Christopher Columbus*. New York: The Viking Press.

Cohen, M. A. (1973). *The Martyr*. Philadelphia, PA: The Jewish Publication Society.

Comay, J. (1980). *The Diaspora Story*. New York: Random House.

David, M. (1933). *Who Was Columbus? His Real Name and Real Fatherland*. New York: The Research Publishing Co.

Graetz, H. (1935). *Popular History of the Jews*. Trans. A. B. Rhine. Vol. IV. New York: Jordan Publishing Co.

———. (1949). *Popular History of the Jews*. Trans. A. B. Rhine. Vol. IV. New York: Hebrew Publishing Co.

Granzotto, G. (1985). *Christopher Columbus: The Dream and the Obsession*. New York: Doubleday.

Kayserling, M. (1968). *Christopher Columbus and the Participation of the Jews in the Spanish and Portuguese Discoveries*. New York: Hermon Press.

"Kol Nidrei." *Encyclopaedia Judaica* (1971). Vol. 10, pp. 1167–1168. New York: Macmillan.

Lea, H. C. (1908). *A History of the Inquisition of Spain*. Vol. I. New York: Macmillan.

Libo, K., and Howe, I. (1984). *We Lived There Too*. New York: St. Martin's/Marek.

Liebman, S. B. (1982). *New World Jewry: Requiem for the Forgotten*. New York: Ktav.

Lindo, E. H. (1848). *The Jews of Spain and Portugal*. London: Longman, Brown, Green & Longmans.

Madariaga, S. de (1940). *Christopher Columbus: Being the Life of the Very Magnificent Lord Don Cristobal Colon*. New York: Macmillan.

Marcus, J. R. (1938). *The Jew in the Medieval World*. Cincinnati, OH: The Union of American Hebrew Congregations.

———. (1955). *Early American Jewry*. Vol. II. New York: Ktav.

Mariejol, J. H. (1961). *The Spain of Ferdinand and Isabella*. New Brunswick, NJ: Rutgers University Press.

Masserman, P., and Baker, M. (1932). *The Jews Come to America*. New York: Bloch.

McEntire, W. F. (1925). *Was Columbus a Jew?* Boston, MA: Stratford.

Minkin, J. S. (1938). *Abarbanel and the Expulsion of the Jews from Spain*. New York: Behrman's Jewish Book House.

Morison, S. E. (1942). *Admiral of the Ocean Sea: A Life of Christopher Columbus*. Boston, MA: Little, Brown and Company.

Netanyahu, B. (1972). *Don Isaac Abravanel: Statesman & Philosopher*. Philadelphia, PA: The Jewish Publication Society of America.

Noveck, S. (1959). *Great Jewish Personalities in Ancient Medieval Times*. Vol. I. Clinton, MA: B'nai B'rith Department of Adult Jewish Education.

Prescott, W. H. (1900). *History of the Reign of Ferdinand and Isabella the Catholic*. Vol. I. Philadelphia, PA: J. B. Lippincott.

Roth, C. (1946). *Personalities and Events in Jewish History*. Philadelphia, PA: The Jewish Publication Society of America.

———. (1969). *A Short History of the Jewish People*. London: Horowitz Publishing Co. Hartmore House.

———. (1974). *A History of the Marranos*. New York: Schocken Books.

Sarchek, J. (1938). *Don Isaac Abravanel*. New York: Bloch.

Schoener, A. (1983). *The American Jewish Album: 1654 to the Present*. New York: Rizzoli International Publications.

Sugar, R., ed. (1973). *Journey of the Fifteen Centuries: the Story of the Jews in Spain*. New York: Union of American Hebrew Congregations.

Walsh, W. T. (1930). *Isabella of Spain: the Last Crusader*. New York: Robert M. McBride & Co.

Wiesenthal, S. (1973). *Sails of Hope*. New York: Macmillan.

Wiznitzer, A. (1960). *Jews in Colonial Brazil*. New York: Columbia University Press.

Zinberg, I. (1972). *A History of Jewish Literature: the Arabic Spanish Period*. Trans. from the Yiddish by Bernard Martin. Philadelphia, PA: The Jewish Publication Society of America.

INDEX

About the Author

Jane Frances Amler comes from a family with traditions of descent from Queen Isabella's personal treasurer, Don Isaac Abravanel. She writes about the history of the Jews in Spain prior to their expulsion in 1492.

Amler was graduated cum laude from New York University, where she received a Bachelor of Science Degree. She earned her Masters Degree from Manhattanville College. The author of two historical novels, *The Fifth Kingdom* and *Children of the Covenant*, she writes and lectures extensively on the Sephardim.

Jane Frances Amler lives in New York with her husband and two sons and continues to write both fiction and nonfiction.